The Careful Teacher

How to Avoid the Pitfalls of the Teaching Profession

Michael Burger

COPYRIGHT AND DISCLOSURES

Edited by Nancee-Laetitia Marin, thelanguageagent.com

Paperback ISBN: 9798592711282

For my mom,
the best teacher I ever had

Table of Contents

Introduction

It was the spring of 2005. My wife and I had a year-old baby boy, and we had just moved into our second home. I was in a career that made me miserable, and I needed to get out. I was an attorney who was unable to find his niche in the legal field. There were many attorneys I associated with who were very content with their chosen field of work. However, being a lawyer just was not as satisfying for me.

My main goal was to be the best dad and husband possible. I knew that being in a career where I was always stressed and unhappy would not allow me to achieve this goal.

So that summer, I decided to switch careers and become a teacher. Many of my in-laws were educators, and it was obvious that they really enjoyed their jobs. Also, I felt like I already knew everything one needed to know to be a good teacher. I had a great amount of experience. If you count my time in college and law school, I spent about twenty years in a classroom. I believed my long and vast experience as a student gave me everything I needed to know to become a successful classroom teacher.

I set the wheels in motion. It was easy. I only needed to pass the Praxis test and take a six-week online class to become certified. I did these in the late spring, and by late summer I had my alternate route license to teach.

Getting my first job was even easier than getting my license. I saw that they were interviewing for positions in a small Title 1 district about a half hour from my home. I interviewed for a middle school math position on a Monday; I was told I got the job on Tuesday. On Wednesday I was in court arguing a case for a friend's client. Thursday and Friday had me in my classroom setting up for the new school year, and Monday was the first day of school for the new students. I literally went from the courtroom to the classroom within one week.

The first day of school was a day I will never forget. My first class came into the room and all the students took their seats. As all my teachers did on the first day of school, I introduced myself and turned around to write my name on the board. While I was writing, I noticed in my peripheral vision an eraser cap flying toward my head. It came from the center of the classroom. I ducked out of the way as the eraser cap ricocheted off the chalk board and bounced onto the floor.

At this point, I had absolutely no idea what to do. This never happened to Sister Mary or Professor Botwinick when they were writing their names on the board. *What do I do?* Instantly I had feelings of panic, fear, and anger coursing through my body. I quickly turned around and looked at the class. Then I thought, *I should do what Sister Mary would do when she got mad at the class – yell!* So I yelled to the top of my lungs, "Who threw that?" Many of the students looked at me like I had three heads. Others had their hands over their mouths trying to conceal their laughter. The student who threw the eraser would not confess, and none of the students would tell me who did it.

Apparently, I yelled so loudly that the head teacher and a staff member heard me down the hallway and came running to my class. I told the head teacher what happened. He quietly asked the class, "Who threw it?" The offender immediately raised his hand. He took the student to the office, and the situation was addressed.

It was at this point that I realized that I knew nothing. Much like eating at a restaurant every day does not give you the ability to run the restaurant, sitting in a classroom for 20 years did not give me the ability to run a classroom. I needed to start from scratch and learn all I could about how to be an effective teacher.

I used many of the classroom management tricks that I read in books and saw in other classrooms. I learned the curriculum up and down, and I began adopting strategies that allowed for efficient and thorough student learning.

Needless to say, I made many mistakes along the way, and even today I am still working to become a better teacher.

As I gained experience, I noticed that there were many in our field, new and experienced, who were great teachers. They were fantastic classroom managers. They knew how to teach the material, and they knew their subject matter up and down. However, they were sometimes oblivious to the fact that their actions would cause stress to themselves and those around them. Their careless decisions would bring about situations where they, their principal, or their students would unnecessarily be put in an unfavorable position.

For instance, there was a teacher in my district who was disciplined for posting negative comments about one of his students on Facebook. There was also a teacher in my school who had the parents of one of her students claim that her practice of peer grading contributed to a bullying incident involving their daughter. There was another incident in my father-in-law's district where a teacher drove a student home from school in violation of district policy and was disciplined by their board of education.

A part of me didn't understand why these teachers, who were all smart people with otherwise great reputations, did not foresee how their actions may have caused these problems. But another part of me completely understood why they did what they did. Saying what he did on Facebook may have been a way for that teacher to vent many of the frustrations that all of us feel as teachers. A teacher's life can be very busy and stressful. Having the students grade the papers may have been a quick and easy way for the teacher to save time. Giving a student a ride home may have been an act of kindness that the student needed at that moment.

Nonetheless, as teachers we have to be careful with our words and actions. We have to make sure that we don't do anything to compromise our reputations or careers. At the same time, we have to do the absolute best we can to make a positive impact on our students. This book will address different instances where we need to be cognizant of our actions. We will also explore alternative ways we can positively impact the lives of our students without damaging our reputations and jobs.

We Have to EAT

Studies show that teachers make over 1,500 decisions a day.[1] Whether we are choosing whom to call upon, or deciding how to approach a lesson, or figuring out how to deal with a disrespectful student, we teachers have to make a myriad of decisions every hour of every school day. As we have seen with the aforementioned examples, it is not beyond the realm of possibility to think that more than a few of these decisions could adversely impact our careers if they are made without proper consideration.

I have noticed that the teachers who tend to make sound decisions and do the right things have a particular mindset: a *careful teacher* mindset. When I spend time with these educators, it is obvious this careful teacher mindset is applied to every decision they make in their professional lives.

These careful teachers' approach to their decision making is defined by three specific qualities:

- First, the careful teacher shows a sense of empathy for others in her decision making.

- Second, when making decisions, the careful teacher thinks two steps ahead and anticipates the impact of her decision down the line.
- Third, the careful teacher tends to be very mindful of how others interpret what she says and does. The careful teacher does what she can to avoid that awkward conversation where she has to try to explain why she made a poor decision.

To be successful teachers, we all have to **EAT**. When making decisions, we need to have **empathy** for our students. We must avoid the **awkward** conversation, and we must always look **two** steps ahead.

Empathy

Empathy is the ability to share and understand another's feelings. Because we are in a position of authority over those who are the most vulnerable in our society, we must always try to empathize with our students when we make decisions that affect them. If we lack empathy in our decisions, we may be putting our students in an unnecessarily compromising and unfair position. Careful teachers are teachers who apply a sense of empathy for their students and other stakeholders in their decision-making.

For example, Joe is a high school teacher. He has a struggling student, Anna, who asks to go to the nurse several times a day. At his school's weekly staff meeting, the teachers and the principal openly speculate over whether Anna was really not feeling well or if she was just trying to avoid class. The nurse made it known that it seemed she was legitimately sick. However, other times the nurse suspected the complaints were not genuine. Some teachers said they would no longer give her permission to see the nurse. In Joe's class the next day, Anna claims she has a headache and asks if she can see the nurse. Joe is pretty sure that she is asking to see the nurse because she wants to avoid completing the exit ticket he has given to the class. Nonetheless, he knows how hard it is to do anything with a bad headache. If by chance she does have a headache, it would be cruel of Joe to not allow Anna to see the nurse and take a couple of aspirin. Therefore, he does not hesitate to give her permission to see the nurse.

Avoid the Awkward Situation

There is nothing more awkward than finding yourself in a position where you are trying to defend a decision that can't be defended. During the course of our school day, when we are making the many decisions we make, it is always a good idea to ask ourselves how others may react if they knew we were choosing to deal with a situation in a particular way. The careful teacher keeps in mind the potential circumstance where she may have to explain to a parent, a student, or an administrator why she made a decision that shouldn't have been made.

For example, Mary is a fifth grade teacher. A student approaches her at the start of the day and asks if he could distribute flyers advertising sign-ups for the local baseball league. Mary knows that any organization needs board approval to distribute any kind of literature to the students. She is not positive, but is pretty sure that the baseball league did not get board approval to distribute the flyers. If she just allows him to distribute the flyers, probably nothing would come of it. She also knows that this particular student would complain and give her a tough time if she tells him no. Even though it may have been easier to allow him to distribute the flyers, Mary tells him he can't distribute them and explains the reasons why. She does this because she doesn't want to find herself in a position where she was having that awkward conversation with her principal trying to explain why she violated board policy.

Think Two Steps Ahead

Many times, we make decisions as teachers that, at the time, seem like the right thing to do. However, down the line we question that decision. For this reason, we must always be cognizant of how our decisions may be interpreted down the line by our students, our students' parents, our coworkers, and our administration. The careful teacher always tends to think two steps ahead when making decisions. The potential for making a regretful decision and having that decision be scrutinized down the line is always at the forefront of the careful teacher's mind.

For example, a middle school math teacher, Ms. Emily, has two students come to her room after school because they need help with math. She also has another student in her room to retake a test, and she has to make a copy of the test for that student. It would be easy for Ms. Emily to leave the students alone in her room for 90 seconds while she goes down the hall to quickly make the copies. Nonetheless, she makes the students walk with her to the copy room. It is not that Ms. Emily does not trust them to be alone in her room. It is the fact that if, by chance, some mischief does occur with the students while they are alone in her room, down the line she may be held partly responsible because she was the one who left them unsupervised.

Book Format

Each chapter of this book will be formatted the same. First, I will give you a common scenario (or scenarios) where a teacher is put in a compromising position. The scenario will involve a situation either where the teacher has to make a tough decision or where the teacher has to deal with the consequences of a decision that has already been made. Many of these scenarios reflect common situations that will occur with a teacher.

I will then discuss the facts of a legal case that parallel the scenario. In most of these legal cases, teachers made decisions where they put their careers in jeopardy. The purpose of the legal case is not to help you understand how the law applies to each situation. In fact, in many of the chapters I do not even mention how the court ruled or what rule of law applied to the case. Whether the teacher won or lost the case is not important. The fact that these teachers put their jobs and reputations in jeopardy because of their own actions is what I want to address. Helping you do the right thing when put in a similar position is the purpose of this book.

After we discuss the case law, we will discuss how to effectively prevent the situation from occurring or deal with the situation in the event it does occur. When giving advice, I will pull from my own experience and the experiences of other teachers. I am hopeful this will allow you to reflect on your own experience and develop your own approach when dealing with the particular circumstance.

Lastly, each chapter will conclude with some short bullet points. The bullet points will address how the scenario could have been avoided if one or more of the three elements of the Careful Teacher mindset was applied. I am hopeful this will help you develop a careful teacher mindset and approach toward your professional decision making.

Supervision

When I was researching case law for this book, there was a common expression used by courts when describing many of the duties associated with being a teacher. The expression was *in loco parentis*. This literally means "in the place of the parent". As teachers, our obligations go beyond teaching the materials in the textbook. Because we are the adult authority in our schools, we have to help ensure the safety of our students. As a parent is obligated to do what she can to make sure her child does not do anything to cause harm to himself or others, we are obligated to do the same with our students. In this section, we will discuss how to protect students when they tend to be most vulnerable.

CHAPTER 1

Supervising the Classroom

Scenario 1

Ms. Chatty is a middle school teacher. Fifth period just ended, and the school day is starting to wind down. There is only one more class left, and it has been a hard day for Ms. Chatty. She had to break up a fight in the morning when the students came into school off the bus. During lunch she fielded a phone call from an angry parent whose child failed his last test. Also, spring break begins the next day, so the students have been more rambunctious than usual. When standing in the hallway between classes, Ms. Chatty often likes to have short conversations with Mr. Gabby, the teacher across the hall.

On this particular day, the two are talking about their spring break plans. The bell rings and all the students are in the classroom. However, Mr. Gabby is just getting started describing the trip he is going to take to Walla Walla. Also, it looks like he has no intention of going into his classroom until he is finished talking. Ms. Chatty is enjoying the conversation and, truth be told, it is nice for her to have a civil adult conversation, considering the day she has already had.

Scenario 2

Mr. Nervous is a high school gym teacher. It has been a good school year for him. He really enjoys all of his classes. However, there is one class where he has a particularly rowdy group of young ladies. During the first and last five minutes of class, it is routine for all of the students to change in the locker room. These girls tend to be loud during these changing times. Oftentimes he hears them arguing with one another. He has done the best he could to deal with the situation, but he obviously can't go into the locker room to monitor the girls. On this particular day, he heard there was a fight during lunch between two of the girls. Mr. Nervous knows it will not be pretty when the girls are changing for gym with no one right there to supervise them.

Case

In *Flanagan v. Canton*, there was a gym class where several students were misbehaving and acting overly aggressive toward one another.[1] The teacher stopped the class and lectured them on the importance of being safe and behaving properly before letting them into the locker room to get changed. Instead of going into the locker room to supervise the boys while they were changing, the teacher stayed outside to talk with a student. During this time, a student was injured when he was violently pushed into a locker. The student sued the school, claiming that the incident would not have occurred if the teacher was in the locker room supervising the students.

In *Cirillo v. City of Milwaukee*, another gym teacher told his students to shoot basketballs after taking attendance. He then left the gym for an undisclosed reason.[2] The teacher was gone for about 25 minutes. During this time, several students began playing a rowdy game of keep away. One of the students was injured when he was pushed to the floor. As in the last case, the student sued the school, claiming that the teacher's absence contributed to him getting injured.

Discussion

I want to say that it is never wise to for us to leave our classrooms unattended. It is easy to find ourselves in a position where, at that moment, the need to be away from our class outweighs our need to be with our class. It may be because we want to finish a conversation with a colleague, or we may need to use the bathroom. Or we may need to get an answer to a question from the teacher across the hallway. It is easy to say to ourselves, "I will just be a minute. Nothing will happen."

However, what if something does happen? How will this look? We need to be cognizant of the fact that if something does happen with our students while our class is being unattended, part of the blame will fall on us. It will be hard to explain to an administrator that our need to run across the hall to borrow printer paper during the middle of our class was the reason why a student got hurt.

This is not so cut and dry when your classroom is more than just one big room. Like in the scenario with Mr. Nervous, how do you supervise a room that you can't go into? How do your monitor students when they are not in your presence?

Clearly, in these situations we have to be more vigilant in our supervision. We can't be in two places at once, but we can be smart about how we supervise students when they are outside our presence.

One strategy is to give a very specific and short period of time for students to do what they need to do when they are outside your presence. A friend of mine is an excellent gym teacher. He gives his students only a few minutes to get changed, and he will stand outside the locker rooms when the students are getting changed and yell how much time is left for them to come out. It is amazing to watch the students hustle to quickly get changed and out to the gym as he counts down the seconds.

Furthermore, if a teacher has a class where the students may be outside the teacher's presence somewhat regularly, he should establish strict, clear rules addressing misbehavior that occurs outside the teacher's presence. In my friend's gym class, if a student is late coming out of the locker room for gym three times, they have to serve a lunch detention. This works very well to deter misbehavior. He very rarely has any problems in the locker room.

Also, teachers need to know exactly what the students are doing and how long it should take to do it when the students are outside their presence. When the students go outside your presence, they should have a purpose, a task, and a time frame to complete that task. If they seem to be taking too long, the teacher needs to check on them.

For instance, if a science teacher is having students pull out equipment from the lab closet for a lab he is having that day, he should be aware how long it should take to do what needs to be done. If it is taking longer than expected, he needs to check on the students.

Lastly, a little common sense always helps. Like in the second scenario, you may have two or three students who are more prone to misbehave when they are with each other. In this situation, any teacher should not hesitate to separate the parties. In Mr. Nervous' case, it may be a good idea for him to have each girl change separately. This may make them late for the lesson, but having a couple of girls start gym class a few minutes late is a small price to pay when the safety of the students is at issue.

EAT Notes

A: Avoid the awkward situation. How will I explain it to my boss if a child gets injured because I was not doing what I needed to do to supervise my students?

T: Think two steps ahead. If I let the students go unsupervised, even for a little bit, could something go wrong? Could someone get hurt? May I be partially to blame?

CHAPTER 2

Watch the Halls

Scenario

Mr. Bombarded is a young middle school teacher. It is the end of fifth period, and he has been running behind all day. Last night his baby boy was sick, and he couldn't get any planning done. He came in early that day to get a jump on things, but he wasn't able to finish putting together all the lessons for the day. He did not get a chance to prepare for his sixth period class. To get ready for his sixth period, Mr. Bombarded has to finish setting up a power point presentation he started preparing during the weekend. It should only take a few minutes. Mr. Bombarded does have a little time to finish preparing his power point presentation between classes. He knows it is the teachers' duty to stand in the hallway and monitor the students between the classes, but usually there are a good number of other teachers in the hallway monitoring the students during this time.

Cases

In *Purzycki v. Fairfield*, a child was tripped in the hallway by another student and fell head first through a mesh window in the exit door.[1] The accident occurred after lunch when the children were exiting the cafeteria and traveling through the hallway on their way to the schoolyard for recess. The school had a policy that during this time, the teachers were to have their classroom doors open so they could partially monitor what was going on in the hallway.

In their ruling, The Supreme Court of Connecticut relied on the testimony of the school's principal who said, "If elementary school children are not supervised, they tend to run and engage in horse-play that often results in injuries." Considering this statement to-gether with the fact that school policy did not require the teachers to fully monitor the students in the hallway, the court concluded that a jury could have found the school to be negligent.

In a similar Connecticut case, a young girl, while walking in the hallway between classes, was hit in the eye and injured by a classmate who was throwing pellets that were used in a prior class to make beanbags.[2] In this instance, the school policy was to have the teachers stand in the hallway between classes. Howev-er, it was noted in the facts of the case that one teacher failed to monitor the halls between classes. The plaintiffs alleged that the teacher's actions in not monitoring the hallway were evidence of negligent behavior on the part of the teacher.

Discussion

When I was researching the case law on this topic, something struck me. I noticed that a good amount of the negligent super-vision cases involved situations where an incident occurred out-side the classroom setting. It sparked my curiosity enough that I actually took note of where and when the incidents occurred in each case. Out of the 35 cases I read involving negligent super-vision, 20 of the cases involved incidents that occurred during recess, between classes, or just before or after the school day.

This is startling considering how the standard school day runs. In your typical elementary school day, there will be students com-ing into the school about ten minutes before the bell rings. There will be a 20-minute recess. Dismissing the students from school will be about a 10-minute process. The rest of the time will be devoted to classroom activity and lunch.

In your typical middle or high school, the students will take about 10 minutes to come in the school, go to their lockers, and get to their first class. There is no recess, but the students will have about three minutes between classes to move from class to class, and the students usually need about 10 minutes at the end of the day to get their things and go home or to an extracurricular activity.

If you do the math, this means that only about 40 minutes a day is spent outside the lunchroom or classroom. Nonetheless, the majority of the cases I read involving negligent supervision occurred during these times. Why is this?

If you are familiar with a typical school setting, the answer is clear. First, these are the times of the day where students are allowed to move around free from the rigors of the classroom. If children are going to misbehave, it will most likely be during these times.

These also happen to be the times of the day where teachers get to interact with other adults. After spending three hours with eight-year-olds, it is nice to have a short respite out in the school yard during recess where we have the opportunity to share our stories, problems, and concerns with other adults who also happen to have recess duty. It is natural for us to put our guard down during this time. We are not as aware of our surroundings as we would be if we were in our classroom.

Lastly, as we saw with Mr. Bombarded, these tend to be the portions of the day where teachers can catch up on things. It is easy to take a minute to send a quick email or print out a copy of a test. If we show up a little late for locker or bus duty, it is usually no problem. Talking for 30 seconds to that student in our classroom between classes is fine because odds are nothing is going to happen during that time anyway.

Nevertheless, we saw in the case law that things could happen. These duties should not be ignored or put off. We should make it a priority to monitor the halls between classes, show up to our before and after school duties in time, and be cognizant of what is going on when we have recess duty. If, by chance, something does occur where a student gets hurt and it happens in front of your room or on your watch, then you may have angry administrators and upset parents coming to you asking what happened.

EAT Notes

A: Avoid that uncomfortable conversation with your principal where you have to account for why you didn't do all you could to make sure the students were safe.

T: Think two steps ahead. If you are not in the hallway keeping an eye out between classes, or if you are not watching your students during recess time, there is a chance that somebody could get hurt. If that happens, it may be partially your fault.

CHAPTER 3

Field Trip Supervision

Scenario 1

Mr. Burdened is a new high school teacher. He was put in charge of this year's freshman field trip to the zoo. It seemed like nobody on the staff wanted to step up and be in charge of the trip. That is why the trip was dropped on his lap. He is worried because last year's trip was an absolute fiasco. Some students were caught throwing things at the animals. Other students were seen running around the zoo, being disrespectful to the patrons. Several people at the zoo, including the zoo staff, approached the teachers and complained about the students' behavior. At the end of the day, one of the students could not be found. It took an hour and a half to find him, which caused the bus to be late returning to school.

Mr. Burdened looked at different options for this year's freshman trip, but the Board of Education will only allow field trips to be taken to certain places. The zoo is the only place on the list that the school can afford, and the principal insists that each class takes one field trip every year. He is forced to organize this trip. He wants to make a good first impression on his coworkers and principal, but he is afraid that this year's trip to the zoo will turn out just like last year's trip.

Scenario 2

Mr. Burdened's wife, Mrs. Burdened, is a middle school teacher. She also has a class trip, but unlike her husband, she is not in charge of everything. Her class trip is to a nearby amusement park. Five students are in her group. It is understood that teachers are responsible for the students in their groups. The teachers and students alike are very much looking forward to this particular field trip. Last year, the students took a trip to a nature reserve. Though it was an informative trip, it was not very fun or exciting. The talk around the staff is that they are going to let the students run around the reserve to do whatever they want. The students are responsible for meeting up with the teachers at the park entrance when the day ends. One of the teachers, a friend of Mrs. Burdened, tells her that she is going to let her group venture through the amusement park unsupervised and asks Mrs. Burdened if she wants to spend the day hanging out with her at the park restaurant.

Cases

In *Glankler v. Rapides Parish School Board,* a five-year-old girl's parents sued the school district when their daughter severely broke her leg on a field trip, causing permanent damage.[1] The young girl was hit by a heavy glider swing while playing in a park. The court found the school to be negligent. The court reasoned that the swings the children played on were too dangerous for five-year-olds. The swings were designed to be used by older children. The kindergarteners could not even touch the ground with their feet when they were sitting on the swing. Thus, the school staff was negligent by allowing the students to play on these swings.

In another more tragic case, an eight-year-old boy drowned on a class swimming trip.[2] The plaintiffs cited several facts that they believe constituted negligent behavior on the part of the school. There were 75 students in the water, and no teachers were in the water with the children. There were not enough supervisors for the number of children who were present. Of the supervisors who stood on the shoreline to monitor the students, none could swim. The school did not screen students to see who could and could not swim. Supervisors were not assigned specific students, and no buddy system was established. Also, no organized system of supervision was established prior to the field trip, and the parents of the child were not even told that there was a class swimming trip that day.

Bell v. Board of Education was a case where a sixth-grade class was on a field trip to a local park.[3] A student asked her teacher if she could go to a pizzeria outside the perimeters of the park for lunch. He allowed her to go to the pizzeria. At the end of the day, when the class was getting ready to board the bus and leave the park, the teacher did a head count and could not find the student. On the way back to school, the teacher actually stopped at the girl's house to tell her mother that she had missed the bus back to school. After the girl had lunch, she realized that she had missed the bus and made her way back to her house. On her way back home, she was attacked and raped by three boys.

Discussion

As you can see with these cases, a great number of things can go wrong when school children are taken on a field trip. If we are running a school trip, there are several cautionary steps we should take to help ensure a safe and headache-free field trip.

First, never take younger elementary school students on a field trip where swimming is involved. Swimming may be fun, but it is also inherently dangerous. It is hard to monitor children in a pool or lake, and it only takes seconds for there to be some kind of accident where a child is severely injured or even killed.

Even if we decide to take older students on a trip where swimming is involved, we should cover our bases and do everything we can to make the trip as safe as possible. We need to make sure the swimming area is well supervised. We should give the parents proper notice as to the time and nature of the trip. Also, we need to make sure that wherever we go, there are other activities the students can partake in that do not involve swimming. We should give those students who are uncomfortable in the water something else to do while on the field trip.

When organizing any school trip, we should set clear boundaries with the students. They should know where they are permitted and forbidden to go while on the trip. Students should also understand any and all expectations with regard to their behavior.

You know you are watching a good lesson when the students are actively engaged. This is also true for field trips. When planning trips, we need to always take the time to make sure the students are actively engaged throughout the day. The less down time you have, the better the chances that the students will not do things that will get them (or you) in trouble.

I remember I was asked to arrange a trip to the Constitution Center in Philadelphia during my first year teaching. It was the first class trip I organized. Ordering the bus, getting the tickets to the Center, and ordering the bagged lunches went pretty smoothly. When we got there, it was a different story. The Constitution Center itself was interesting and informative. There were exhibits and information that we teachers found very interesting. However, the students didn't find the museum nearly as interesting. Throughout our stay at the Constitution Center, I found myself constantly wrangling students who were wandering off and stopping students from horse playing in the middle of the museum.

The next year, the powers above agreed that we should take the same trip. I knew that we had to do this differently. We decided to turn the trip into a scavenger hunt. Prior to the trip, a couple of teachers and I went to the Constitution Center on our own and wrote down facts that were displayed with the exhibits. Using this information, we wrote a scavenger hunt list of information the students needed to find. The students who found the most information would win a student prize pack.

As it turned out, this was an excellent idea. The kids were fully engaged, scurrying back and forth throughout the center, trying to find as much information as possible in hopes of winning the prize pack. It also made our jobs easier. We didn't have to tell students to stop horse playing, and we didn't have to chase kids down who were going places they weren't supposed to go. Also, the students learned a great deal about our Constitution and the place it had in our history. We kept that scavenger list and used it every time we took a trip to the Constitution Center.

No matter where we decide to go, we should also make sure we have enough chaperones. This will often mean having other teachers and parent volunteers come on the trip. We want to make sure to have a list of teachers' and chaperones' cell phone numbers in the event they need to be contacted during the course of the trip. If we are in charge of a group of students, we should get a list of cell phone numbers of all the students in the group, in the event we are in a crowded place and we lose them.

If we are in charge of a group of younger students, we should make sure they are with us during the entire trip. However, if we are in a place where we can let our group walk around freely and we have older students, it is a good idea to have them meet at a rendezvous point at specific times. By doing this, we can keep track of our students without having to constantly follow them around.

Also, be sure to communicate with parents about when the students should be picked up. With many field trips, the students may not arrive back to the school until after the school day ends. If the students need to be picked up, it is important that the parents know what time they need be there to pick up their child. We do not want to find ourselves waiting for a student's parent to pick up her child two hours after the buses come back from the trip.

EAT Notes

E: When on a field trip, have empathy for parents who are entrusting us with the care of their children. Many parents, especially parents of younger children, probably would not feel comfortable having their young child go on a school trip where they were allowed to run around unsupervised.

A: Avoid the uncomfortable conversation with a parent or your principal where you have to explain why something occurred on a trip that put a child in danger.

T: Think two steps ahead. Understand that something can go wrong if you do not do what you need to make sure the students are properly supervised on a class trip. It may come back to you if your students are left unsupervised in a strange place on a school trip.

Chapter 4

The School Bus

Scenario

Coach Norman Dale is the assistant coach of a high school basketball team. The team had a very good season and made it to the championship game. Coach Dale is on the bus going to the game with the head coach and the team. The head coach usually sits in the front of the bus, and Coach Dale usually sits in the back. The kids have been particularly rowdy on this trip. Coach Dale has already told certain students to calm down and behave several times.

The head coach hasn't even noticed any of the misbehaving students because he is engrossed in drawing up some plays that may work well against their opponent. While Coach Dale is sitting in his seat at the back of the bus, the head coach turns around and calls him, asking him to come to the front of the bus and review the game plan. Coach Dale feels uncomfortable leaving the back of the bus because the students are more likely to do something they will regret if he is not nearby monitoring their behavior.

Case

In *Doe v. DeSoto Parish School Board* the plaintiff, a 16- year-old-girl was on a bus traveling to another school with her school's boys and girls basketball teams.[1] While on the bus, she was sexually assaulted by five members of the boys' team. The incident went unnoticed by the teams' coaches who were on the bus during the assault. The court upheld the jury's verdict against the school district, holding them liable under a claim of negligent supervision.

In discussing the coaches' negligence, the court cited an important fact. The coaches did follow school policy when they had the boys and girls teams sit in different sections of the bus. However, they were also required to sit between the two sections. Both coaches in this case sat in the front of the bus. Also, despite the argument that the plaintiff consented to the sexual contact, the court said it could have been prevented if the coaches were more diligent with their supervision of the students.

Discussion

During the course of the school year, almost all teachers find themselves on a bus with students for one reason or the other. If we are on a school trip or if we are taking our team to an away game, we will be in a situation where we are supervising a large group of children as they are being transported to some destination.

In my experience, many teachers' approach toward supervision on a school bus is like my approach toward central air-conditioning maintenance. I live in the state of Delaware. In this part of the country, we experience the four seasons. We have cold winters and hot summers. We will only run our central air conditioner continuously for about four months of the year. They recommend that we get our central air conditioning units serviced every spring to make sure our system is in good running order.

During the spring I was (and still am) at my busiest. I was helping coach my two sons' baseball teams, and our school usually had a great deal going on during this time. Needless to say, I would always forget to have my central air unit serviced. This wasn't a problem for years because I would just turn on my central air conditioning when it got hot, and it would cool the house with no problem for the duration of the summer.

One warm spring day a couple of years ago, it was time to kick on my central air-conditioning system. I quickly noticed that there was no cool air coming through the vents. I called a repair person to come to my house and fix the unit. It turned out that I had to pay a good amount of money to make some major repairs to my HVAC system. The repairman told me the problems that existed in my air conditioning unit could have been prevented if I just would have had somebody service it every year.

I learned my lesson the hard way. I now have a service person come to the house every spring to do the necessary routine maintenance on my air conditioning unit.

Many in our profession approach student supervision on buses like I approached the maintenance needs of my air conditioning unit. They take the occasional school bus trip, sit with other teachers in the front of the bus, and don't recognize the potential dangers of not sitting in an area where they can properly supervise their students. Most of the time, the trips on the bus go without incident. However, as with my air conditioning system, one day something may go wrong. A student may get hurt, and we may be partly responsible.

As with the scenario and the case, you can very easily find yourself partaking in these bad habits. Students tend to sit with the members of their group. So do teachers. Let's face it—on a bus, the only person a teacher can have a mature conversation with is another teacher, so it is natural for teachers to sit with each other. However, as we have seen, doing this can compromise the duty we have to supervise our students in a proper and effective way.

Unlike the teachers in *DeSoto,* we need to be cognizant of what is going on with the students at all times. It is a good idea to make it clear to the students that they need to stay in their seats for the duration of the trip. Also, take the initiative to separate the students who tend to be a bad influence on others and don't hesitate to make sure that the student or students with discipline issues are sitting close to you. Furthermore, teachers need to be strategic regarding where they sit.

We can more easily monitor the bus if we put ourselves in a position where we can see what is going on. Making sure we periodically walk up and down the aisle to check on our students never hurts. For long trips, it may be a good idea to treat the bus like a classroom. Give the students games or activities that will keep them engaged during the trip. Games work well to keep children quiet and focused on something while on the bus. Something as simple as giving the students a brochure of the museum or park they are going to will help engage them for a short period of time. If they are going to a large amusement park and you know the students will not be able to enjoy all the park has to offer, you may want to give the students a blank itinerary they can fill out while on the bus.

It is easy for us to see the bus as a break. We are not in a classroom. There is no lesson, and we are usually taking a trip to a fun place or event. Nonetheless, because of these factors, we need to be diligent when monitoring our students' behavior.

EAT Notes

A: Avoid the uncomfortable conversation with your principal where you have to explain how you didn't notice students misbehaving on the bus.

T: Think two steps ahead and understand that if a student does something wrong on the bus and you were not actively supervising at that time, some of the blame may lie with you.

After School

Many of us are involved with school-related activities that occur after the school day is complete. Whether it is managing the school paper, coaching the school's basketball team, or running the Spanish club, we often have duties that exist after the final school bell has rung.

This is a nice way for many of us to earn a little extra money. It is also a great way for us to build bonds with our students. I coached my school's track, basketball, and football teams. I also coached my school's math league team. The fact that I was outside the classroom in a more relaxed atmosphere with my students allowed me to build stronger relationships with these students.

Because we were in a more relaxed atmosphere, it was easier for me to let my supervisor guard down. I found myself at times not being as careful as I normally would be if the students were with me in a classroom setting. We will discuss situations where students were harmed after school because the adults who were responsible for their safety let their guard down.

CHAPTER 5

Leaving Students Alone after School

Scenario

Mr. Rocky Andahardplace is the new teacher and coach for his middle school's basketball team. He has a good team this year, and he really enjoys coaching. It seems like he always has somewhere to be or something to do after the school day. He has practice after school every day until 5 p.m. When Rocky gets out of practice, he has to run to pick up his daughter from daycare. The daycare is only open until 6 p.m., and they have strict rules regarding picking children up on time. He has pushed it to the last minute a couple of times since the season began.

On this particular day, it is already past 5:30 p.m. Practice has ended and Rocky needs to get out of school to pick up his child. However, Rocky is still waiting for one of his players to get picked up by his parents. He tries calling the parent, and there is no answer. It is getting dark and the school is not in a safe area, so Rocky does not want to leave the student alone. Rocky is also thinking about just driving the student home, but there is a strict school policy that forbids teachers to drive students in their cars. His wife is still at work. He can't get a hold of her anyway because she is in a late meeting. Rocky needs to do something because he is running out of time.

Case

In *Broward County School District. v. Ruiz*, the plaintiff, Ruiz, just finished taking team pictures with his junior varsity football team.[1] After the pictures were taken, the coach took several players out to practice with the varsity team. Ruiz stayed behind and waited in the cafeteria to be picked up by his father. While waiting in the school cafeteria, Ruiz was assaulted and beaten by three other boys. Ruiz sued the coach and the school for negligent supervision.

The court found that the junior varsity coach's behavior was not negligent for the reason that he would have had to leave his team behind in order to stay with Ruiz. However, it did find there to be enough evidence for the school to be found negligent by a jury. This was because the school did not have any staff stationed to monitor the cafeteria after school despite the fact that several students congregated in the cafeteria every day after school.

Discussion

When running after school activities, we are still obligated to supervise and keep the students in our charge safe. As we saw in the case, we still have a duty to make sure our students are not put in a position where they may be unnecessarily harmed.

The circumstance may arise where we are at the school with a student waiting several minutes or hours for his parents to pick him up. As we already know, leaving students alone *during* the school day is not an option. Therefore, it should go without saying that leaving students alone for extended periods of time *after* the school day is not an option either.

Driving a student home in your car is probably not a good idea. It is not wise for us to put ourselves in a position where we are alone in a confined place with a student for a long period of time. (We will discuss this scenario in more detail in chapter 17.) Also, many school districts and schools have policies forbidding teachers to drive students in their cars.

Coaches and teachers who run after-school programs should be aware of their school's practices and procedures when situations like these arise. If no rules are in place, we should take the time to talk with our principal about the expectations when such an incident does occur.

There are several measures we could take to avoid finding ourselves in the same predicament as Mr. Andahardplace in the scenario.

It may be a good idea to establish some kind of consequence if parents are habitually late when picking up their child. I know coaches who will suspend a player or not allow a player to play a game if their parents are tardy a certain number of times. Let the parents be aware of the policy from the beginning. Sending a tardiness policy statement home with the player and having the parent sign it is always a good idea.

One may think it is unfair to establish rules that punish a child for his or her parents' behavior. However, I speak from experience when I tell you that this is a necessary and effective rule to set in place.

In my first year coaching, I did not establish any rules addressing this issue, and I paid the price. I specifically remember one student's parents. They were habitually late picking up their child. As the season wore on, their tardiness got worse and worse. At first, they were regularly five to 10 minutes late when picking her up. By midseason, it was not uncommon for them to be a half hour late. By the end of the season, there were several occasions where they were almost an hour late. At times, I would respectfully remind them that practice was over at 5:30 p.m., and that was the time that their daughter was to be picked up. They would smile and apologize, but the next day, the same thing would happen again.

Meanwhile, my schedule was becoming even more strained. In a typical day during the sports season, I would wake up at 5:15 a.m., get ready, and drive one hour to work. I would do some planning and grading, then classes would begin. The school day would end, and I would start practice at 3:30 p.m. Practice would go until 5:15 p.m., and the team would be ready to go home by 5:30 p.m. The times when this player was picked up an hour late, I wouldn't be able to leave until about 6:30 p.m. I would drive an hour and arrive at home by 7:30 p.m. I would eat dinner by myself because my family would have already eaten. Then I would spend about a half hour with my wife and two boys. After the boys went to bed, I would plan and grade until about 11 p.m., and then go to bed. The next day, I would do it all again.

As you can see, the wasted hour prevented me from spending important time with my family. This schedule is not uncommon for anybody who teaches and coaches. Just ask somebody who does it. Many teachers who coach already have demanding schedules that allow for little spare time. They do not need to be wasting time sitting with a player waiting for the parent to pick them up.

If parents have problems getting to the school to pick up their child in a timely manner, they should make arrangements with the school to have another person pick up the child. This is why I believe it is not unfair to expect parents to pick their children up on time and to have consequences in place in the event this does not happen. If we plan to coach or do any after school activity while teaching, I would advise to also set a policy in place that motivates the parents to be on time when picking up their child.

We also might want to ask the parents for an updated list of all numbers where they can be reached. Do not rely on the school administrative office to give you the set of contact numbers that they have in their files. People often change their cell phone numbers. Many people do not notify the school when they change their phone number. It may be a good idea to have the parents fill out a form where they give you their most up-to-date contact information.

It goes without saying that we should run these ideas by our principal before we take any of these precautionary steps.

Lastly, do not be afraid to ask the principal for his or her personal phone number in the event something does occur where you might need their assistance. A good principal would want to be contacted in the event something happened and a student could not be picked up from school.

EAT Notes

E: Empathize with parents who do not want their children left alone after school by a coach or teacher.

A: Avoid the uncomfortable conversation with your principal or parents when you have to explain to them that students were harmed because you left them alone.

CHAPTER 6

Passing a Child to the Right Person

Scenario

Ms. Inapickle is an elementary school teacher. This year she is in charge of directing the school's annual Christmas play. The students rehearse for the school play every day during school hours. However, with the play only a week away, Ms. Inapickle is now also having rehearsal after school. One particular day, the after-school rehearsal finished at 5 p.m. By 5:15 p.m., all but one student, Rebecca, were picked up by their parents. By 5:30 p.m., Ms. Inapickle and Rebecca were still waiting for her parents to arrive.

Up until this day, her parents were always on time. This time, though, a young man about 18 years of age drives up to the front of the school, hops out of the car, and tells Ms. Inapickle that he is Rebecca's neighbor and he was sent by her parents to pick her up. Rebecca's dad was taken to the emergency room because he had pains in his chest, and Rebecca's mother was at the hospital with her father.

Case

In the case of *Baker v. Clay*, a mother sued a school district for allowing her child to be picked up and taken from the school by an unauthorized person.[1] The facts that led to the plaintiff's claim were discussed in detail.

A woman came to the school and approached the secretary. She told the secretary that she wanted to pick up a child. She indicated on the sign-out sheet that she was the child's father's cousin. The secretary was not suspicious because the boy recognized her when he arrived to the office. The secretary did not check the release form that was filled out by his natural mother to see whether this woman was authorized to take the child. Also, no instruction or guidance was given to the secretary with regard to how to verify whether a person was authorized to take a child. Tragically, the boy was murdered shortly after being picked up. The woman who picked him up and his stepmother were charged with the crime.

The court addressed whether a specific federal law applied to the case and did not give an opinion regarding the substantive facts of the case. Nonetheless, the facts serve as a cautionary tale to anybody who works in education.

Discussion

Most of us who have responsibilities to students after school at the high school level do not have to deal with these issues. At this age, the students are more independent. Many have driving licenses or have friends who have driving licenses. Making sure the student gets picked up from practice by the right person is usually not a serious concern for high school teachers.

If we are in charge of after-school activities at the middle or elementary school level, it is a different story. I believe many teachers would have no problem letting a younger child leave with the neighbor or with another family member if they were in the same position as Ms. Inapickle or the secretary in the case. It makes sense. If circumstances are the same, 99.9 percent of the time, the child will be fine. The child will be safe if they leave school with a cousin or family friend. However, as we saw in the case, if something does occur the consequences could be absolutely horrifying.

You can liken this situation to the need to wear a seat belt. When my children hop in my car, I make sure that they clip on their seat belts. They probably have driven in my car thousands of times, and not one time did I get into an accident. Nonetheless, I still make sure they wear their seatbelts. I do this because if, by chance, we do get into an accident, they could get seriously injured or even killed.

We should take the same approach to the present scenario. Granted, nothing will probably happen if Ms. Inapickle just lets the student leave with the neighbor. However, the potential harm can be catastrophic if something does happen. Therefore, we should take some necessary precautions.

First, it is important to know your school's rules and customs. There already may be a policy or a protocol established for teachers to follow if parents do not show to pick up their child. If you are a new teacher or if you are new to running an after-school program, you will want to ask your principal what to do in these circumstances.

Outside of following an established school policy, it is always a good idea to send a letter home to parents. The letter can address what the parent can do if they are unable to pick up their child.

The letter may also include a section where the parents can list other people who are allowed to pick the child up from school. Usually, your school would have a similar list on file where backup contacts are listed in case of emergency. Nonetheless, having an updated emergency list is always a good idea. It may also be wise to leave a number with the parent so they can call you in the event of an emergency. As we have already stated, if you decide to send a letter to parents, you should always run it by your administrator before sending it.

Finally, as we noted in the last chapter, it is always good to have the parents' and your administrator's phone numbers readily available in the event you find yourself in this situation.

EAT Notes

E: Empathize with parents and do what you can to make sure their children are safe when they leave you.

A: Avoid the uncomfortable conversation with a parent where you try to explain why you allowed their child to leave with somebody who did not have permission to take the child.

CHAPTER 7

Keeping a Student after School

Scenario

Mr. Ari Tated is a teacher at Central High School. He has a student in his class named Thomas. Thomas is a nice young man, but he talks entirely too much in class. He isn't malicious or sneaky. He just has a penchant for striking up a conversation with those around him at the most inappropriate times. Thomas's habitual talking has gotten him in so much trouble that he has been put in the school's lunch detention for the next few weeks. Generally, when a student gets in trouble, he will be written up by the teacher and have to serve a lunch detention, where he eats lunch in a quiet place isolated from his classmates.

Most of the students at the school take the bus home, so no policy exists where students can serve an after school detention. Some students walk home. Several times teachers have held these students after school for one reason or the other, but the teacher was responsible for watching the student who was serving the detention.

One day Thomas is being particularly chatty in Mr. Tated's class. Mr. Tated has to ask Thomas to stop talking six times. To make matters worse, it seems like Thomas gets louder each time he is asked to be quiet. Mr. Tated's frustration grows each time he has to ask Thomas to stop talking. He wants to issue Thomas a lunch detention but knows that it will have little effect since Thomas is in lunch detention for the next few weeks. He also knows that

Thomas is one of the few students who walks home from school. When Thomas strikes up a conversation for the seventh time, Mr. Tated reaches his breaking point and tells Thomas that he has to come to his class at the end of the school day to serve an after-school detention.

Case

Perna v. Conejo Valley Unified School District is a case where a teacher asked a twelve year old student to stay after school to help him grade papers.[1] The student and her older sister stayed after school until 3 p.m. to help the teacher. On their way home, the girls were struck by a car at a busy intersection and sustained injuries. A crossing guard was always stationed at that intersection after school, but by the time the girls got to the intersection, the guard had already left for the day. The parents of the girls sued the school, seeking compensation for their injuries.

The school argued that they could not be negligent because the accident occurred after school and off school grounds. The California appellate court disagreed with this argument. The court reasoned that the teacher knew or should have known that the crossing guard would not be on duty at that time. By holding the girls after school, his actions could be seen as a "proximate cause" of their subsequent injuries. Thus, a jury could find the teacher and the school negligent based on the facts.

Discussion

The end of the academic workday is not the end of the day for many students. Whether partaking in extracurricular activities, helping teachers organize their classrooms, or just serving a detention, a good number of students often stay on school grounds long after the bell rings. As we have seen in the case, we need to make sure that a student's safety and well-being is not being compromised if we have her stay after school.

If we have a child stay for any reason, we need to contact the parents before we have the child stay after school. We should not just send an email. It is wise to make sure we call the parents and leave messages until we contact them. If we cannot reach the parent, we may want to schedule it for a later date. It may be time consuming, but we do not want to be the cause of any unnecessary anxiety on the part of the parents.

Also, if we are giving a child detention for bad behavior, we should touch base with the parents to let them know of the issue we have with their child. It is always a good idea to also let our principal know if she gets a phone call from the parents to discuss the reason behind the detention. This not only applies to grade school students but also to middle and high school students. No matter what the grade level, most parents and principals will appreciate the teacher contacting them to tell them that a child will not be home at normal time because of their behavior.

With reference to Mr. Tated's situation it may have been wise for him to tell Thomas that he was to serve the detention after school a subsequent day after Mr. Tated contacted Thomas's parents.

If we believe that we may have students stay after school during the course of the school year, it may be sensible to establish a contact procedure with the parents. Most teachers send home an introduction letter or syllabus for parents to sign and return. It may be a good idea to indicate that we may have a student stay after school in this letter home. Also, have the parents give you the primary number where they can be reached during the school day. This may help you save time when calling the parents. As always, before we establish any kind of personal policy or protocol, make sure to reference your school policy and get your principal's permission.

I remember one day I told my class that I had to hang some student-made posters in the hallway after school. One of my students, Carlos, raised his hand and asked if he could help me with hanging the posters. I often had students volunteer to stay, but Carlos wasn't one of them. I knew Carlos walked home and did not have to take the bus. I happily allowed him to stay to help me put up the posters.

After school Carlos showed up in my room, and we began putting up the posters. After about 20 minutes, I looked down the hall and noticed a very angry-looking woman walking toward Carlos and me. It was his mother. She yelled at him and told him to immediately go to her car. She then told me that he had a dentist appointment and he was supposed to come home immediately after school. I apologized for not contacting her to get her permission to have Carlos stay. She told me that he hated going to the dentist and did what he could to avoid it. Apparently, Carlos's volunteering to stay came more from his need to avoid the dentist and less from his desire to help his teacher.

No matter what the reason may be, having a student stay after school is commonplace in any school. Whenever we have a student stay after dismissal, it is always wise to contact the parents, and make sure that we do not put the student in a position where his or her safety is at risk.

EAT Notes

E: Have empathy for parents and notify them if their child is staying after school for any reason. You don't want them to worry if their child doesn't come home on time.

A: Avoid the uncomfortable conversation that I had with Carlos's mom when she came after school to get her son and I found myself apologizing for not contacting her.

T: Think two steps ahead and consider the possibility that the student may have another obligation or commitment before you hold him after school, or, like in the case, you may be jeopardizing his safety by sending him home through unsafe conditions.

Student Expression

School should be a place where children should have the freedom to express themselves in a manner where they feel comfortable and free from judgment. A classroom culture where students are engaged in the learning process and feel like they can express themselves within that process is ideal. However, we have to make sure that expression does not come at a cost. Our students should be allowed to express their opinions in a constructive way, and these opinions should be received in a fair and respectful learning environment.

Students also have a right to express their opinions outside the classroom. The cyberworld we now live in gives all of us, including our students, various platforms where our thoughts can be publicized. Whether it is on their own website, social media, or on a Rate Your Teacher website, students now have the power and right to make public their opinions of us as people and teachers.

In the next three chapters, we will discuss how to allow students to express themselves in a positive and safe environment. We will also talk about how to address the situation where the teacher may be the victim of student expression.

CHAPTER 8

The Pledge of Allegiance

Scenario

Ms. Patriot is a high school teacher. She has a student from Palestine named Suraiya. Recently, there has been a great amount of violence between the Israelis and the Palestinians, and the President of the United States just had a press conference where he backed the Israelis and condemned the actions of the Palestinians. This greatly upset those in the Palestinian community in the US. One morning, during the Pledge of Allegiance, Ms. Patriot noticed that Suraiya stayed in her seat and faced her body away from the flag. After the pledge, she approached Suraiya and asked her why she did not participate. Suraiya told her that because of the recent stance the US took in the Palestinian-Israeli conflict, she is refusing to take the Pledge of Allegiance.

Case

In *West Virginia Board of Education v. Barnette*, a West Virginia state law mandated that all students were to face the flag and recite the Pledge of Allegiance.[1] If students did not participate, they could be expelled from school, and the parents could even lose custody of their children. A group of Jehovah's Witnesses, who believed that reciting the Pledge of Allegiance was akin to idol worship, challenged the law, saying it violated their First Amendment rights. The Supreme Court held that compelling students to salute the flag and recite the pledge did indeed violate their rights.

49

Thus, if a student refuses to recite the Pledge of Allegiance, he has a right to do so.

Justice Brown, who sat on the court, said, "If there is any fixed star in our constitutional constellation, it is that no official, high or petty, can prescribe what shall be orthodox in politics, nationalism, religion or other matters of opinion or force citizens to confess by word or act their faith therein."[2]

Discussion

I do not want to get into a debate regarding the constitutionality of the court ruling, nor do I want to get into the specifics regarding how different states and districts approach this issue. I do want to discuss how to approach the situation if it happens to you.

This has never happened to me, but I know several teachers who have had students refuse to take the Pledge of Allegiance. Before it happens to you, you should probably find out what the school district policy is regarding protesting the Pledge of Allegiance. It won't take much time to look up the policy in the district handbook, or ask your administrator how to deal with the situation if it does occur.

If you do ask your administrator, you will probably be told to just ignore it and allow the student to remain seated during the Pledge of Allegiance. We should remember that the student may be bringing negative attention to himself from the other students. You will need to take steps to help protect the student from being bullied by other students who may be offended by the protest.

Do not bring attention to a student who is choosing not to involve herself in the pledge. Talk to her privately and tell your principal as soon as conveniently possible, especially if the student is doing it for a political or religious reason. Also, if it is concluded that the student can refuse to recite the Pledge of Allegiance, then try not to have the student do it in an area where she may be teased or confronted. Have the student sit away from anybody who will take offense to it. If students find it offensive in any way, you need to remind them that it is their right to not take the Pledge. Remember, further action can be taken with help from your principal if it is disrupting the educational process.

EAT Notes

E: Have empathy for the student who is refusing to take the Pledge of Allegiance. Do what you can to prevent any bullying that may come as a result of the student's refusal to take the pledge.

A: Avoid the uncomfortable conversation with the parent you will have when you explain to them why you forced his or her child to take the Pledge of Allegiance.

T: Think two steps ahead. Consider the possible turmoil that can come from forcing a student to say the Pledge of Allegiance.

CHAPTER 9

Student Expression in Class Papers

Scenario

Mrs. Vague is a high school history teacher. She just finished a weeklong unit on the Kennedy presidency. The lessons touched on everything from his debates against Richard Nixon to the Cuban Missile Crisis to the Kennedy assassination. Mrs. Vague decided she wanted to give an assignment where the students write about an event from the Kennedy presidency. She told the students to write a 500-word essay detailing any event from the Kennedy presidency.

The next week Mrs. Vague graded the assignment, and she came across a paper that was written by one of her more colorful students named Danny. It was titled "Happy Birthday, Mr. President." The essay detailed the affair Jack Kennedy had with Marilyn Monroe. It was very well written. If it wasn't for the topic he chose, it would have been an easy A. However, Mrs. Vague didn't think the topic was appropriate. She called Danny aside and told him he would have to pick a more legitimate topic that was based on an issue that was discussed in class.

Daniel got very upset and told her that they did spend several minutes talking about the affairs President Kennedy had with different women. She explained to him that even though there was a short side conversation about Kennedy's exploits with women, this had nothing to do with his policies or the events from his presidency. Danny told Mrs. Vague that he felt he shouldn't have to redo it because when she gave the assignment, she only required that it address a topic that was discussed in class.

Case

In *Lacks v. Ferguson Reorganized School District*, a schoolteacher allowed her students to put profanity in their writing assignments.[1] The principal found out about this practice and told her to stop allowing the students to use profanity in their papers, as it violated the school's profanity policy. The teacher ignored the policy and the warnings from the principal and continued to allow the students to use profanity in their work. Eventually, the school district fired her for violating their profanity policy. The teacher sued the school district, claiming that this violated her First Amendment rights. The court disagreed. They stated that a "student's First Amendment rights in schools and classrooms must be balanced against the society's countervailing interest in teaching students the boundaries of socially appropriate behavior."[2]

Discussion

I remember my first year as a teacher. I was teaching a unit on similar shapes. In geometry similar shapes are two shapes with the exact same shape but a different size. I gave the students a project where I provided a drawing of a bridge, and they had to redraw a larger geometrically similar shaped bridge. When I gave the assignment, I told the students they had to make a similar bridge. One student, Naomi, was very excited to do the project because her father, who was rarely home, was going to be home to help her with it.

A couple of weeks later, I collected the assignment. Each student brought in a scaled drawing of the bridge. Many students put a great amount of effort into the project. Most did a great job, and they were very proud of their work.

Naomi was particularly proud. Instead of bringing in a drawing of a similarly shaped bridge, Naomi brought in a three dimensional model made of wire and papier-mâché. You can immediately tell it took hours to build. When she gave it to me, I told her how impressed I was. She told me how great it was having her father help her with the project. It was obvious she was very proud of her work and enjoyed the time she was able to spend with her father working on the project.

There was one problem. The purpose of the project was to have the students display their understanding of similar geometric shapes. To assess their understanding, I had to measure different sides and angles of their drawing. Though her three-dimensional model was amazing, it wasn't geometrically similar to the model in the drawing. When she gave it to me, I told her that they had to be similar. She responded by telling me that the picture I provided was very similar to the model she built. She was right. It was similar in the common use of the word, but it was not geometrically similar.

I was stuck between a rock and a hard place. Naomi gave me a project that didn't warrant a good grade because it wasn't geometrically similar to the drawing I provided. Nonetheless, she did work hard on it, and she did follow the only real direction I gave the students, which was that it had to be "similar." In the end I redid the project with her after school. The grade I gave her was based on what we did together. She didn't understand why I was making her draw the bridge like everybody else. I let her know that I thought her work with her dad was great, but I just wanted to make sure she understood the material.

The case, the scenario, and my own story all have a common message. When we give large assignments, we need to make clear the expectations involved in completing the assignment. If we don't make the expectations clear, we may be inadvertently putting ourselves in a compromising position.

A good way to address this is by giving the students a guideline sheet that sets out all expectations of the assignment. If we are giving a project that may be similar to the one Mrs. Vague gave in the scenario, we may want to include the specific topics that could be addressed. Much like with the case, if we work in a district or school where they have certain rules that must be followed in completing a project, we may want to include those rules in our guidelines to make sure the students adhere to them.

It may also be a good idea to put your grading rubric in the guideline sheet. Also, I have seen teachers hand out sample A-grade work so students know what a quality project or paper looks like. Making our expectations clear will help our students better understand what they need to do to be successful. It also helps us avoid potential future headaches when grading the assignment.

EAT Notes

E: Have empathy for the students. Like with my situation, you don't want to put yourself in a position where a student gets a bad grade on a project because your directions were not clear.

T: Look two steps ahead and think what may happen if some students misinterpret the directions given on a project or paper.

CHAPTER 10

Cyberbullying of Teachers

Scenario 1

Mr. McFly is a middle school math teacher at Hill Valley High School. He has a student in his class named Biff who is very bright but also very disruptive. Biff knows a great deal about computers and has helped some teachers with their work-related computer problems. Biff has also helped set up websites for the school sports teams and school newspaper. Mr. McFly and Biff never really hit it off. Mr. McFly wrote up Biff several times for being disruptive in class, and Biff has made it known that Mr. McFly is his least favorite teacher.

One day a student approached Mr. McFly and told him that Biff started his own website titled Why My Math Teacher Sucks. The site had several Photoshopped pictures of Mr. McFly. In one picture, he was wearing a court jester's outfit, and another picture had him sitting on a stool wearing a dunce cap. The site also had a page that listed the Top Ten Reasons Why Mr. McFly Sucks, which included inappropriate suggestions regarding Mr. McFly's sexual preference and social life.

Scenario 2

Mr. Rooney is a new high school teacher. It is halfway through the first year and he feels he is acclimating well to his new environment. The principal likes Mr. Rooney. He is respected and liked by the other teachers, and the students seem to enjoy Mr. Rooney's class. One day he was searching online and found a site where students make comments and rate their teachers. He found his name on the site with several student comments. The comments were not flattering. They claimed Mr. Rooney was an extremely irresponsible and uncaring teacher.

Case

In *Killion v. Franklin Regional School District*, a student composed a top ten list criticizing the school's athletic director and sent it in an email to his friends.[1] The top 10 list included statements that were lewd and cruel. The items in the list made fun of his weight and contained inappropriate remarks regarding the size of his genitals. A copy of the list was found on school grounds and brought to the principal. The student was given a 10-day suspension. The student sued the school, claiming that the suspension violated his First Amendment rights. The court reasoned that, though it upset the athletic director, it was something that was made outside school and was not substantially disruptive to the school environment.

J.S. v. Bethlehem was a case where a student designed a website that posted pictures of a teacher's severed head dripping with blood.[2] The site also had a page where it tried to procure the services of a hit man to murder the teacher and listed reasons why she should die. The existence of the site was known by staff and students at the school. The teacher was so emotionally distraught by the site that she had to take a leave of absence from her position. When they learned of the website, the school suspended the student for 10 days.

The student and his parents sued the school district, claiming that the suspension violated his First Amendment rights. Testimony from staff and students indicated that the website harmfully affected the morale and culture of the school. The court found that, because it materially and substantially interfered with the education process, the school officials were justified when they suspended the student.

Discussion

Cyberbullying is the use of electronic media to bully a person. As we have seen, students can use electronic media as a means to bully their teachers. Cyberbullying of teachers can take different forms. It can be done through texting, blogs, emails, social media, and websites.

As we all know, students can make comments about teachers on social media or blogs. Sometimes these comments are caustic enough to be considered cyberbullying. Even if it isn't considered bullying in the strictest sense of the word, these comments can be unfair and hurtful.

I had a student who wrote some negative comments about me on one of those "grade your teacher" websites. The student, who was anonymous, also made negative comments about every other teacher who taught him that particular year. When I saw the post, I was alarmed and hurt. A couple of things he said were constructive criticisms. Other things were embellished misperceptions or just not true.

I consider myself to be a good teacher and an open-minded person. I take what I do seriously, and I am very approachable. I was hurt that the student never came to me about any of these issues during the school year. He obviously had issues with his teachers. The internet was not the fair or appropriate way to vent these issues. He should have told the teachers or the principal so that the issues could be resolved.

When I went to school the next day, I was still upset. However, it didn't take long for me to realize that I was being oversensitive.

I had my post-observation meeting with my principal, who told me it was clear to him that the students enjoyed my class and were all actively engaged in learning. A student approached me that morning and told me that she really enjoyed my class and that I had a way of making math "easy."

As teachers, we are not able to make all of the students happy with us all of the time. Sometimes, it is our jobs to be stern or do the unpopular thing to help better our students. Considering the number of children who use social media on a regular basis, you should not be surprised to find a negative comment or two written about you on the web. If the negative comment was reasonable, try to learn from it as you would try to learn from any other constructive criticism given to you. If the criticism is not true or unwarranted, remember that we are dealing with children, many of whom do not yet know how to express themselves in a mature and appropriate manner. Therefore, we should be professional and try to take the unfair criticism in stride.

There are several ways in which students can use electronic media to harass, embarrass, and intimidate their teachers. As we have seen in the cases and the first scenario, students have set up websites to attack and hurt their teachers. There are also several cases where students have stolen a teacher's online identity to humiliate them. There are also incidents where students have sent harassing messages to teachers via texting, email or social media.

To prevent similar incidents from happening to you, it is a good idea to make sure that you do not give any personal information to students. This includes phone numbers, personal email addresses, and home addresses. Also, it is always good practice not to make friends with or follow students on any kind of social media like Facebook or Twitter.

If you think you are the victim of cyberbullying, you should first report it to your principal. As we have seen in these cases, they may not be able to discipline the student because they may consider the issue outside the perimeters of the school and not interfering with educational process. If your principal cannot do anything as far as suspending or disciplining the student, you may consider calling the parents and asking them to address the problem with the child.

You may also be able to contact the internet or social network provider and have them take down the site, pictures, or comments. For instance, Facebook has a safety center that allows users to report bullying to Facebook.

If you still cannot remedy the situation, you may have to take legal action by either calling the police and/or calling an attorney. If you do this, it is wise to keep your administration and your union abreast of what you are doing.

Remember, the world is much more different today than it was just twenty years ago. Thanks to the internet and modern technology, people can very easily present their feelings regarding another person to millions of people. As teachers, we have to remember that we have a duty to maintain a sense of professionalism when we feel we are being treated unfairly through the cyberworld. Nonetheless, if the criticism reaches inappropriate or dangerous levels, we should not hesitate to address the problem through our administration or even legal means if necessary.

EAT Notes

T: Think two steps ahead. If negative comments are posted about you on the internet, think about the lives of the children you will touch in a positive way. Don't let the actions of one person or a small group of people weigh you down.

Know the Policy

It is the last day of summer. The kids come in tomorrow for their first day of school. We have to report to school to set up our classrooms and attend the annual beginning of the school year meeting. At the meeting the principal hands us a copy of the teacher and student handbooks. Most of us find a nice drawer to put them in with the idea we will review the handbooks sometime soon. We never do.

As teachers, most of us are busy people with little spare time to do things like memorize sections and subsections of the school rules. However, we have to remember that we are expected to follow and enforce many of the rules addressed in those handbooks.

With this in mind, we need to review the rules and make an attempt to familiarize ourselves with those items that bear upon our everyday responsibilities as teachers. I will discuss some situations where teachers put themselves in compromising positions because they ignored school policy and procedure.

CHAPTER 11

Following the Dress Code

Scenario

Ms. Una Ware is a new middle school teacher. She is only a few months away from finishing her first year of teaching. The weather is getting warm and spring is in the air. It is the beginning of a busy day. There is a big test the next day, and Una has to review an important unit with her first period class. The kids start streaming into class. As the students are entering the class, Una notices a young lady named Susan who is wearing a half-shirt that shows her midriff. Immediately, Una begins to think that this attire may violate the school dress code. She remembered getting a copy of the dress code and putting it somewhere in her file drawer, but she didn't really have time to search for it. She could send Susan to the principal's office to have the principal check, but this time of the morning is always extremely busy in the office. It may take half the class for the principal to even see Susan. If it doesn't violate the dress code, then Susan would have missed half the review for no good reason.

Case

In the case of *Guiles v. Marineau*, a student came to school wearing a shirt described below:[1]

> The front of the shirt, at the top, has a large print that reads "George W. Bush," and below it is the text "Chicken-Hawk-In-Chief." Directly below these words is a large picture of the president's face, wearing a helmet, superimposed on

the body of a chicken. Surrounding the president are images of oil rigs and dollar symbols. To one side of the president, three lines of cocaine and a razor blade appear. In the "chicken wing" of the president nearest the cocaine, there is a straw. In the other "wing" the president is holding a martini glass with an olive in it. Directly below all these depictions is printed "1st Chicken Hawk Wing," and below that is text reading "World Domination Tour."

The back of the T-shirt has similar pictures and language, including the lines of cocaine and the martini glass. The representations on the back of the shirt are surrounded by smaller print accusing the President of being a "Crook," "Cocaine Addict," "AWOL, Draft Dodger," and "Lying Drunk Driver." The sleeves of the shirt each depict a military patch, one with a man drinking from a bottle, and the other with a chicken flanked by a bottle and three lines of cocaine with a razor.

The student wore the shirt in school about once a week for a couple months before he was told it violated the school's dress code. The student sued the school claiming that his First Amendment rights were violated when the school told him he was not allowed to wear the shirt.

The court agreed with the student and ruled that the student did have a right to wear the shirt in school. The court reasoned that the student was allowed to wear the shirt because when he did wear the shirt, it did not cause any kind of substantial disruption to the school environment.

Discussion

As teachers, we have many responsibilities. Our typical workday is usually full. We spend most of our day teaching classes.

Those moments when we are not teaching, we spend planning, grading, or monitoring students. Understanding and enforcing the dress code is not always at the top of our list of things to do. Nonetheless, it is important that we enforce the school rules.

It is a common situation. We notice a student wearing something that kids typically wear, but it violates school code. At that moment, it may feel like the benefit of enforcing the dress code is outweighed by the burden of taking the time to do what needs to be done to enforce it. So we choose to ignore it and move on with our day.

However, as we saw with *Guiles v. Marineau*, ignoring a dress code violation may harm us in the end. Not to say that ignoring the dress code will lead to some big lawsuit, but it may eventually give you some headaches when it is all said and done. For instance, let us say Ms. Una Ware in the scenario decides not to do anything. The next day, Susan comes in again wearing the same half shirt. The principal sees Susan on that day and makes her call home for mom to bring in a new shirt because the half shirt violated the dress code. Mom comes in, visibly upset, with a new shirt in hand. She explains to the principal that Susan was allowed to wear that shirt before, and it makes no sense that she is not allowed to wear it again. Clearly, by ignoring the school dress code, Ms. Ware puts the principal in an uncomfortable position with a parent. This probably means she will find herself in an uncomfortable position with the principal.

I make it a point to enforce the dress code. If your school dress code is like mine, it is pretty detailed. I cannot memorize it. Nor do I have the time to memorize it. However, I do know what parts of the dress code are most commonly violated. Also, I make it a point to have a copy of the dress code in my desk in the event I have to refer to it. It may seem like a waste of time to review your school dress code or to take the time to make a copy of it and put it in a place that is easily accessible. Nevertheless, taking these steps may prevent problems from occurring in the future.

EAT Notes

E: Have empathy for the principal who needs her staff to be consistent when enforcing the school rules to efficiently and effectively run a school.

A: Avoid the uncomfortable discussion with your principal regarding why you are not enforcing school dress code policy.

CHAPTER 12

Giving Homework

Scenario

Mrs. Tarea is a new high school Spanish teacher. She just graduated from college, and this is her first job. She really lucked out. Despite the fact she had no teaching experience, Mrs. Tarea landed a position at a very good school close to her home. The school had virtually no behavior problems, and it was rated very high academically compared to other schools in the state.

Mrs. Tarea is trying to establish a homework policy for her students. She really has no idea what she should do regarding homework. She wants to regularly assign homework, but she just has no idea how much homework to assign, when to assign it, and what to assign.

There are two other foreign language teachers in the school who Mrs. Tarea sees as mentors. One of these mentors is Ms. Taskmaster. She regularly gives an hour of homework a night. She tells Mrs. Tarea that to learn in her class, the students need to practice every night. The other teacher, Mr. Minimal, rarely gives homework. Mr. Minimal explains to her that he doesn't want to overload the students, and he considers the students' time in class their practice time. He also said that he only wants to give homework that he could review with the class. If the students are given a great deal of homework, there is no way he would have the time to review all the work during class.

There is a school policy that does not allow teachers to give more than 30 minutes of homework per night for each subject. When she asked Ms. Taskmaster about this, she told Mrs. Tarea that some of her advanced students can finish the homework in about 40 minutes, which is close to a half hour. Also, the students' parents very much consider Ms. Taskmaster to be a better teacher than Mr. Minimal. They generally feel that the students learn more in Ms. Taskmaster's class because she gives more homework.

Mrs. Tarea wants to make a good impression with the parents, but she doesn't want to compromise the school rules. Also, she genuinely sees both teachers' points behind why they give the amount of homework they do. She is not sure what to do.

Case

In *Gilliland v. Board of Education*, a school dismissed a teacher for being incompetent and the teacher sued the school to try to get her job back.[1] In their defense, the school cited many reasons for firing the teacher. Among those reasons was the fact that the teacher commonly gave three and a half to five hours of homework a night to her second grade class. She was also accused of not giving clear instructions when assigning work and giving work that was meant for students who were two or three grade levels ahead.

Discussion

When I was a young elementary and middle school student in the late 70s and early 80s, I regularly had homework. In math class, I remember always having to do a bunch of practice problems. Usually, the assignment was to do a group of problems from our textbook. The teacher would have us do all the odd problems from the lesson because the even problems had the answers in the back of the book. I remember when I understood the math, the homework was very monotonous and time consuming. If I had trouble understanding the math, the homework was frustrating.

In classes like science and social studies, the assignment was usually to read a section from the textbook then answer the questions at the end of the section. I remember the better students always had it complete and correct. Most of these students had the advantage of having parents who would make sure they had their answers right. The average students would often have it complete but would have some wrong answers because their parents weren't as diligent in checking their work or couldn't check their work. The struggling students often didn't even do the assignment, or, if they did do it, the assignment was done at the last minute, and they literally guessed the answers.

In my opinion, language arts was the worst. A common homework assignment had us reading chapters from a classic fiction book. During class, there were really never any lessons that addressed the content of the book. It was expected that we learn the book at home. At a certain point, we were supposed to have finished the book, then we were tested on it. Much like with the other subjects, the high performers usually had their parents read the book with them. The average students read the book but didn't really get much of the book because a good amount of it was over their heads. The low students often would not have read the book at all. By test time, it was clear who was going to get the A and who wasn't.

Today the world is different. Since that time educators have become a little more understanding of how a student's home life may affect his academic performance. Also, research has shown that homework often does little to aid in student learning.[2]

Please don't get me wrong; I am not against giving homework. We just have to be more thoughtful in how we give it. Many school districts have rules that state time limits on assigned homework. Unlike Ms. Taskmaster, we should follow these rules keeping in mind our average and struggling students. Having a student work by herself for an extended period of time on subject matter she doesn't really understand only makes the learning process more frustrating for her.

When assigning homework, we should make sure it is doable, unlike the teacher in *Gilliland v. Board of Education*. It is also a good idea to give the students time to come to you and get assistance if they need it. In my class, I will assign a handful of review problems for homework. I will always give one or two weeks for the students to complete it. The students can submit it to me whenever they finish. As the due date approaches, I will remind students that they still owe me the homework. If the due date is within a day or two, I will often give the student a lunch pass or an after-school pass so he can come to my room and work on the homework with my help if necessary. This ensures that everybody does the homework. It also ensures that everybody has the opportunity to get a little help if they need it.

When assigning homework, we need to be considerate of the school rules and the resources our students may or may not have at home. Homework needs to be a tool that contributes to student success, not inhibits it.

EAT Notes

E: Have empathy for the student and their parents. It may not be feasible to expect students and parents to understand and finish an assignment in a reasonable amount of time.

T: Think two steps ahead. If I give the students an assignment, will the assignment help the students better understand the material, or will students become more frustrated and confused with the material?

CHAPTER 13

Grading Policy

Scenario 1

Ms. Calculate is a language arts teacher. Her school mandates that no more than 10 percent of the grade can be devoted to everyday classwork. Ms. Calculate established a grading system where her tests and projects were worth 20 points each and quizzes were worth 10 points each. She collects a warm-up every day and gives a daily classwork grade. Because classwork grades can only amount to 10 percent of the total grade, Ms. Calculate makes sure to make each daily warm-up worth only one point. She recently submitted her grades for the first marking period.

One day shortly thereafter, Ms. Calculate was asked to speak with the principal about her grading system. He pointed out that she had 40 classwork grades that marking period totaling 40 points. He also noted that she had a project grade, a test grade, and two quiz grades in the book. These added up to 60 points. Even though she only made each classwork grade worth one point each, these grades amounted to 40 percent of her total grade, which violated the school grading policy.

Scenario 2

Mr. Fluff is a fourth grade teacher. He has several categories in his grading system. Mr. Fluff has an organization grade worth 10 percent of the total grade. He also has a participation grade worth 15 percent. Classwork is worth 20 percent, and homework is worth 15 percent. Assessments, like tests and quizzes, make up 40 percent of the grade.

Mr. Fluff gets a call from an upset parent whose child has done very well on all the tests and quizzes. However, her child received a C in math because his participation and organization grades were very low. The parent argues that it is an unfair grade because the district policy stated that all grades must be standards-based. The parent claims that a child's ability to organize and willingness to participate have nothing to do with the math standards.

Case

Keen v. Penson is the only case in this book involving a conflict between a college professor and his student.[1] The case hits the point of this chapter so well that I could not leave it out. *Keen v. Penson* documents the relationship between an outspoken college student and a stubborn professor who did not get along. At the end of the semester, the student unexpectedly received an F in the class. The reason her grade was so low was because she received a zero for class participation. No other participation grade in the class was below a 70. It was clear that the grade was given because the professor did not like the student. The grade had nothing to do with her actual performance in the class. In response to this, the college administration demoted the professor and cut his pay. The professor unsuccessfully sued the university to gain his position and salary back.

Discussion

It is important that we remain cognizant of any grading policy our school may have. Many schools have maximum percentage requirements for certain types of grades. For instance, it is not uncommon for a school or district to have a policy where home-work can only be 10 percent of the total grade. We have to make sure we do not fall into the same trap Ms. Calculate fell into. If we grade on a total point system, we have to make sure the total points for each category fall within any grade percentage man-date our school may have. If you have any trouble figuring out the math, see the math teacher in your building.

Also, many schools are now adopting policies that grades must be standards-based. This kind of requirement can be interpreted different ways. My district has this policy, and I understand it as a requirement that the grades we give have to reflect our stu-dents' understanding of the content in the standards in the sub-ject we teach. In other words, unlike Mr. Fluff and the professor in the case, our grades should not be based on assessments that have nothing to do with the curriculum.

For instance, participation grades often reflect how outspoken or shy a student may be and not necessarily reflect what they know about the material being taught in the class. Likewise, an orga-nization grade may reflect how neat a student is, but it does not show how well he has mastered the content of the class. I am not saying we should ignore these qualities. I am saying it may be a good idea to have these qualities recognized and addressed in places other than the grade book.

Even if we work at a school that does not have a standards-based grading policy, I believe it is wise to make sure the students' grades reflect their understanding of the material. We may have concerned parents who have a child with a low grade and feel that we may be treating their child unfairly. Explaining to par-ents that the grade comes from low test and quiz scores shows that the grade was given without bias, whereas telling parents that their child received a low grade because his notebook was not organized or because he didn't raise his hand enough may lead the parents to believe that we were not objective when assessing their child's performance.

EAT Notes

E: Have empathy for students who work hard to understand the material but may get a bad grade for reasons that have nothing to do with the understanding of the content being taught.

A: Avoid the uncomfortable conversation with your principal where you try to explain why you are violating district policy regarding how much weight should be allocated to one type of grade.

Be Aware

As stated earlier, research shows that teachers make over 1,500 decisions throughout the course of a school day.[1] That is a decision every 15 seconds. Because we make so many decisions, we often find ourselves in a position where we make a judgment that feels right in the circumstance that exists at that moment. However, if we take a step back and look at that decision from a different perspective, we may find that it was the wrong decision.

In the next several chapters, we will examine four different circumstances. Each one will have almost nothing to do with the other. The only thing the cases have in common is that in every circumstance, a teacher made a choice that felt like the right thing to do at that moment, but ultimately, it turned out to be the wrong choice.

CHAPTER 14

Student Bathroom Use

Scenario 1

The school year is beginning to wind down. Finals are in a couple of weeks, and the kids are more rambunctious than usual. It is mentioned at a staff meeting that a specific group of girls have been seen hanging out in the bathroom during class time. The staff concludes that the girls must be agreeing to go to the bathroom at a specific time and then meeting there to socialize. Certain members of the staff want to ban those specific girls from using the bathroom during class time. The principal recommends to only allow them to use the bathroom if they look like they "really need to go." All the teachers agree that this is probably the best way to approach the problem.

The next day, Mr. Piddle is teaching his third period class when Katelyn, one of the girls who was getting out of class to socialize with her friends, raises her hand and asks if she could use the bathroom. She looks like she needs to use the bathroom. However, he doesn't want to let her go because it would not look good if she is going to socialize and the principal sees her out during class time. Nonetheless, Mr. Piddle feels guilty about not allowing a student to use the bathroom. He has always let students use the bathroom, and he doesn't feel right telling her she can't use it.

Scenario 2

Mrs. Tinkle is a second grade teacher. Emily, a student in her class, asks to use the bathroom the same time every day. At around

10 o'clock, just when the students begin their warm-up for math, Emily raises her hand and asks to use the bathroom. She spends five to ten minutes in the bathroom and then comes back to class. She usually misses the warm-up and the part of the class where Mrs. Tinkle models how to do a particular math problem. Emily has been struggling in math lately. Mrs. Tinkle feels that it is because she is consistently missing the beginning of class.

Case

In the case of *Boyett v. Tomberlin*, a high school student, who was suffering from diarrhea, stood up at the beginning of his seventh period class and announced that he needed to use the bathroom. The teacher denied his request.[1] Five minutes later, the student again stood up and loudly announced to the class that he needed to use the restroom. The teacher again denied his request. Ignoring the second refusal, the student left the class and went to the bathroom. In the prior class period, the student showed no signs of discomfort and did not request to use the bathroom. Also, just prior to the incident, the student walked right past the bathroom to the class where he spent a good few minutes talking to his girlfriend before the bell rang.

The student sued the school and the teacher. He claimed "pain and suffering, embarrassment, humiliation and invasion of privacy."[2] The court decided in favor of the school and the teacher. In his reasoning the judge stated, "that argument begs the question, which, for the classroom teacher, is: does the student genuinely need to use the restroom, or is he seeking to get out of class for another reason? A teacher's resolution of that question necessarily involves an exercise in judgment and choice. It is the epitome of a discretionary function."[3] In other words, because the student may be lying about his need to use the bathroom, it is within the teacher's discretion to allow or disallow the student to use it.

Discussion

This is one issue where you will often find that there is no school-wide policy that all teachers must follow. Usually, it is within the teacher's discretion to deal with student bathroom use as she sees fit. In my experience, I have seen teachers who almost always deny permission. This is usually because they believe that students have the opportunity to use the bathroom before school or at lunch and should not use class time to take care of these issues. Other teachers are very free and open with allowing students to use the bathroom. They will give permission to anyone who asks.

In my opinion, a teacher should never have a patent rule not allowing students to use the bathroom during the class. There are several reasons behind this. First, you never want to put a student in a position where an accident could occur in your classroom. This can cause an immense amount of embarrassment and psychological damage to a young person. Whether it is a first grader who might be trying to avoid class or a senior in high school who you feel may want to smoke a cigarette in the bathroom, I believe they should be given the benefit of the doubt.

Also, a student is not able to perform to her ability if she is trying to concentrate in class while also trying to deal with the discomfort of having to use the bathroom. I would rather have a student leave the class for five minutes and be at her best to learn in my class for the remaining 40 minutes than have a student in my class for the whole 45 minutes, suffering with a discomfort that will impede her ability to learn.

Lastly, I have empathy for anybody who needs to use the bathroom but cannot for any reason. I remember when I was in the third grade. I was in school with some stomach issues and asked my teacher if I could use the bathroom. For whatever reason, she told me no. I was too afraid to ask again or plead with her to allow me to go. I sat for at least two hours in absolute pain and discomfort. I remember doubling over and holding my stomach as I was running home after school to use the bathroom. It took me about twenty minutes to walk home from school. It was one of the most torturous moments of my life. I am sure most people have similar stories from their childhood where they had to relieve themselves, and somebody would not allow them to do so. The fact of the matter is that I do not want to be the person whose decision inflicts this kind of discomfort on another human being.

A teacher should never absolutely deny a student the right to use the bathroom unless she is sure that the person does not really have to use it. No teacher wants to find herself in a position where she is sitting in the principal's office trying to explain to her boss and the child's parents why she did not allow a child to perform a natural bodily function.

This being said, we do not want to be that teacher with a caravan of students going in and out of our room during our class. There are ways to allow students to use the bathroom without having a situation where the students are taking advantage of us and missing valuable class time.

To deal with this, many teachers establish certain ground rules that they follow in their class. At the beginning of class, when my students are filing in, the students who truly have to go to the bathroom will quickly approach me so I can give them permission to use the bathroom, which I will do immediately before or at the beginning of my class.

If there are students in my room well before the bell and they happen to be students who frequently ask to use the bathroom, I will often tell them that they should take advantage of the extra two minutes before class and use the bathroom before the class starts. If the teacher in the case did this, he may have prevented the lawsuit from occurring.

Also, when students ask me for permission to use the bathroom, I will often tell them that they can go. However, they have to wait a few minutes so we can finish a portion of the lesson. They then can ask me when that portion is finished, and I will let them go. It is always just a few minutes, so they're not greatly inconvenienced. What I like about this practice is that it usually shows whether they need to use the bathroom or not. Sometimes they don't ask again, which tells me that they didn't really have to go. More often than not, they'll raise his hand at the appointed time and ask again for permission to use the bathroom. At this point, I will always let them use the restroom.

This method would have worked in the first scenario. If the teacher just asked Katelyn to wait five minutes, it would have put a damper on her plans to have a bathroom rendezvous with her friends. Also, it would have given her the opportunity to use the bathroom if she really had to use it.

If we suspect that a student may be taking advantage of us, we may need to contact the parent. I remember I had one student who would always need to use the ladies' room at the beginning of my class. Because she was the first to ask and it was the beginning of the class, I would always allow her to use the bathroom. She always struggled in my math class, but when she began to make her daily trips to the ladies' room, her grades got worse.

I thought she might be avoiding the challenging warm-up questions that I often put on the board at the beginning of the class. I also believed that this just might be the time of day that she needed to use the bathroom. I called her parents and told them that I thought her failing grade was partly due to her missing the first five minutes of the class. My recommendation was that she try to use the bathroom during the last five minutes of lunch. The end of lunch was about 50 minutes before the beginning of my class. She began doing this and no longer asked to use the bathroom at the beginning of my class. Her grades went up, and the problem was solved.

This solution may have worked well for the teacher in the second scenario. Oftentimes a phone call home and a slight change in the daily routine will help remedy the problem.

Remember, as teachers we have a great amount of authority and influence. Our decisions can have an enormous effect on the lives of our students. No decision of ours should put any student in a position where they needlessly suffer pain or embarrassment. Nonetheless, we cannot put ourselves in a position where we are allowing students to miss important class time. As we have seen, a well-thought-out approach and sound decision-making will usually address these issues.

EAT Notes

E: Have empathy for the student who may be uncomfortable in class because you are not allowing her to use the bathroom.

A: Avoid the uncomfortable conversation with the parents who are upset that their child had an accident in your room because you would not let their child use the bathroom.

CHAPTER 15

Use of Social Media

Scenario

Mr. Whine is a high school teacher. He works at a rough school with an overabundance of discipline problems. Needless to say, the school is a very stressful environment for teachers and administrators alike. The teachers' lounge tends to serve as the place where teachers go to vent their frustrations to other teachers. Mr. Whine likes to go there during his planning period for a few minutes to grab a cup of coffee and talk with some other teachers. The frequent talks have allowed him to become close with these teachers. A couple of them are Facebook friends. One day they mention to Mr. Whine that they will send him a friend request on Facebook.

That night, Mr. Whine is on his Facebook page. He sees the requests and accepts their invitations. He notices that three of the teachers are having a discussion. The conversation is similar to the discussions they have in the teacher's lounge. The teachers are complaining to each other about a specific student's behavior. They are also grumbling over some administrative decisions that were recently made. Mr. Whine wants to chime in, but he feels strange discussing his work issues on Facebook.

Case

Ms. O'Brien, a first grade teacher in New Jersey, was fired for making some insensitive statements on Facebook.[1] After a frustrating day of work, she communicated on Facebook that she wasn't a teacher but a "warden for future criminals."[2] She also stated that she should have brought her first grade class to the Scared Straight program that was in the school that day. News of these statements got out and upset many staff and parents within the district. There was even a small protest held by several parents outside her school.

The school removed her from her position for conduct unbecoming of a teacher. She appealed the school's decision in court. The Superior Court of New Jersey upheld the decision of the school. In its opinion, the court stated that the statements made on Facebook were personal and not of public concern. The court stated that even if the statements were of public concern, "her right to express her views was outweighed by the district's need to operate its school efficiently."[3]

Discussion

The comments made by the teacher in the last case are stronger and more reprehensible than comments most teachers would make about their students. However, remember that many comments we make to family or friends in conversation are meant for only our family and friends. Many of us talk to our spouses or close friends about our jobs and say things in confidence that may be taken as harmful or offensive if heard by others. We should all understand that when we say something on social media, it could be read by more people than we intend. There are many stories out there about people who lost their jobs because of comments they made on social media. We shouldn't put ourselves in a position where we are posting things on social media that we wouldn't want others not close to us to read. If we use social media, we should always try to avoid saying things about our job or saying anything that may put us in a compromising position with our employer.

My wife and her friends use Facebook a great deal. She will often post pictures of me and our children on Facebook. Because I am a teacher, I am aware that a good number of people know me or know who I am. I am also aware that, because of my position, I am an exemplar of proper behavior in my school community. For this reason, I am very sensitive to what kind of pictures of me are posted on social media. I try to make sure that my wife and her friends do not post pictures of me drinking alcohol or doing anything that may be seen as improper or unprofessional.

EAT Notes

A: Avoid the uncomfortable conversation with your principal or superintendent where you have to explain why you posted something on social media that you shouldn't have posted.

T: Think two steps ahead. You may have shared the comment with only your friends, but what if one of your friends thoughtlessly shared the comment with a person who would get upset by it?

CHAPTER 16

Giving Food to Students

Scenario

Mrs. Mars is a first year teacher at Hershey Elementary School. It is a few months into the school year, and she is slowly acclimating to her new job. She has some discipline problems in her classroom, but for the most part, things are going well. She has to observe different teachers several times throughout the year as part of the new teacher program set up by her district. During one of the observations, she notices that a small group of students is beginning to talk and come off task. The teacher stops the class and tells them that there will be no reward at the end of class if their behavior continues. Immediately, they stopped talking and got back on task.

Half an hour later, the class ends, and recess is about to start. As the students put their books under their desks, the teacher walks around and puts a Hershey's Kiss on each student's desk. The students quickly eat their candy and go out the door to recess.

Mrs. Mars asks the teacher about her practice of giving candy to the class. The teacher told Mrs. Mars that when she was a novice teacher, she also had some problems with classroom management. When she started using candy to motivate the students to perform, she saw immediate results.

Case

In *Soter v. Cowles Publishing Company*, an elementary student named Nathan went on a class trip.[1] Nathan had a severe peanut allergy. Brown paper bag lunches consisting of peanut butter sandwiches and a peanut butter cookie were packed for the students. The school staff did not request a special lunch for Nathan. After opening his lunch, Nathan noticed the peanut butter and jelly sandwich and returned it to his teacher, but he ate some of the cookie before he realized it had peanuts in it. Soon thereafter, Nathan had a severe reaction to the cookie and had to be rushed to the hospital. Tragically, Nathan passed away that afternoon.

In *Pace v. State*, a young kindergarten student who also had a severe peanut allergy was given a peanut butter and jelly sandwich by a cafeteria worker.[2] The student told the cafeteria worker that she was not allowed to eat the sandwich. The cafeteria worker ignored her and instructed her to eat the sandwich. The girl followed the cafeteria worker's orders and consumed the sandwich. It did not take long for the girl to get sick. She was rushed to the hospital from the school in an ambulance. Luckily, the girl survived the incident.

Discussion

As we have seen with the two cases, we need to know if any of our students have a severe food allergy or diabetic condition. It is always a good idea to take precautionary measures when planning a trip or event where the students will be consuming any kind of food. A list of students who have food allergies or blood sugar issues should be made available to you. Nonetheless, if one isn't provided, asking the school nurse for a list prior to the trip or event is always a good idea.

Food is often used as a means to help motivate students. Many teachers and schools have some kind of reward system in place to encourage good student behavior. At times, I have seen candy work as an effective motivator. Nonetheless, we need to be careful when giving food to students for any reason.

In recent years, federal and state laws have been passed requiring that schools follow certain nutritional guidelines with the food they serve their students. Students now eat much healthier school lunches than I did during the '70s and '80s. Schools are no longer only responsible for the academic needs of our children, but they are also responsible for making sure our students receive proper nourishment. Since schools now take responsibility for making sure our students make healthy choices, it wouldn't make sense for us, as agents of our school, to give our students candy and cookies in our classrooms.

It should be noted that many districts and schools are now adopting policies that forbid teachers to give students certain kinds of food. We need to be aware if our school has such a policy and make sure we follow that policy if it exists.

Also, we may not want to give food to our students because we often do not know if the parents would permit their children to have that particular food. Many parents do not allow their children to eat different kinds of sugars and carbohydrates. Likewise, many students are on special diets to help treat conditions like asthma or hyperactivity. Allergies aside, when we give students food in our class, we are presuming that the parents would be fine with their child eating that food. We may have an upset parent on our hands if we give their child something to eat at school that she is not allowed to eat at home.

If I was at a party and somebody's child came to me and asked me for a cookie, it would be natural for me to ask the parent if it was okay for the child to have the cookie. Why wouldn't I take the same approach in my classroom?

For these reasons, I believe we should not regularly give food to our students.

I occasionally do give out items, not food, to help motivate my students. When a student does well on a quiz or has a particularly good class, I may give him an eraser or a pencil. I do not do it every day, and I only do it when students go above and beyond their normal performance. Small erasers and pencils can be obtained in bulk for a very cheap price. It doesn't do a lot of damage to my classroom budget. As a math teacher, this helps me because I am giving students something that they need to be prepared for my class.

EAT Notes

E: Have empathy for parents who may not want their child eating certain types of food. Giving their children food that they are not allowed to eat would be disrespectful.

A: Avoid the uncomfortable conversation with the principal when he finds out you are violating a school policy by giving students candy.

T: Think two steps ahead. What if the student gets some kind of allergic reaction to this food? The student may get sick, and you may be to blame.

CHAPTER 17

Student-Teacher Relationship

Scenario

Mr. Ron Popular is a new high school teacher, fresh out of college. Since he was a boy, Ron wanted to be a teacher. As a high school and college student, he admired those teachers who were popular with the students. He always wanted to be like the cool teachers he had when he was in school.

Four months into his first school year, Ron began to notice that he was not the most popular teacher in the building. In fact, he was quite unpopular among the students. The language arts teacher recently gave an assignment where students had to write a thank you letter to their favorite teacher. Ron didn't receive one letter. Also, one of Ron's less tactful students recently told him that she and her friends didn't like his class at all.

Ron is friendly with another young teacher named Mr. Alldarage. Mr. Alldarage is quite popular. In fact, he was the teacher who received all of those thank you letters from the students. The students really like him. Between classes, the boys always high-five him, and the girls often stop to give him a hug as they pass by. He jokes around with the students all the time. Many of his jokes push the perimeters of appropriateness, but this is why the students like him so much. The students also talk to him about their personal lives. He always knows who is dating whom and where the big party is that weekend. Recently, Mr. Alldarage had several students come to his apartment to hang out and play video games. The word is spreading around the school about how much fun the kids had over his place.

Case

The case of *Doe v. Tippercanoe* involved a situation where a teacher was accused of forming an inappropriate relationship with a teenage student.[1] The teacher and the student had a relationship that was clearly beyond what is considered to normal for a teacher-student relationship.

The facts from the case show that the teacher would often have lunch with the student alone in his office. They often spoke on their phones and texted each other, and they also exchanged emails with each other. On occasion, he would take her out for lunch in his car, and she would sometimes come to his house to hang out outside school hours. It was noted that he would often greet her with a hug inside his room and the two would often flirt with each other.

During the time of their relationship, the teacher was going through a divorce. He would often confide in the student, sharing personal information with her regarding his marriage. She would also confide in him about her own family issues. At one point, the two were so close, the teacher actually asked the student to go on a family trip with him to see his daughter.

The teacher was convicted by the court on charges of child seduction.

Discussion

In my opinion, this is the most important chapter of the book. Of all the topics I address in my presentations to teachers, teacher impropriety is the one that sparks the most debate. We all agree that developing inappropriate relationships with students is patently wrong. The debate lies in where that line of impropriety is drawn. At what point does a teacher go too far when developing relationships with students?

I know of teachers who were wrongly accused of acting inappropriately with students. Even though they were able to prove they were innocent, the damage they suffered was extreme. Having to deal with the parents, administration, and the court system proved to be an unbelievable burden. Also, even after proving themselves innocent, it caused irreparable damage to their reputations and careers.

Because of this, we must always approach the individual relationships we have with our students with extreme caution. When the line between appropriate and inappropriate behavior is drawn, we should not even approach that line. In fact, to be safe, we must make sure our behavior stays as far from that line as possible.

Let us look at the teacher's behavior in the case and the scenario. It may seem innocent enough. You tell a joke to a 17-year-old. It is the kind of joke that you usually only hear in a bar. To be honest, the 17-year-old has probably heard jokes like that before. Also, the 17-year-old, because he has the maturity of a 17-year-old, may think you are pretty cool if he hears you tell that joke. Nonetheless, we have to remember that we are teachers. We are the exemplars in our community. The bond we build with our students should be more of a parental bond than a friendly bond that may exist between peers.

In the case and the scenario, there were teachers sharing their contact information with students. We also saw teachers inviting students over to their homes. It may be innocent enough. We are trying to build a strong relationship with our students. Sharing our personal contact information with them, befriending students on social media, or inviting them to our homes allows us to be there for them if they need us for any reason. It also shows them that we are willing to give them our time.

Nonetheless, we must also consider how this may look to others. Putting ourselves in a position where we can interact more personally with students on a social level may allow for the perception that something inappropriate is happening.

We must also be careful with the amount of affection we show our students. I am not saying we need to be cold and uncaring toward them. I am just saying that we have to be aware of how our displays of physical affection may be perceived. Sometimes we need to show some level of physical affection. There is clearly nothing wrong with an elementary school teacher giving a hug to a student or letting a kindergarten student sit on her lap during reading time. However, even the elementary teachers need to be cognizant of how their displays of affection may be perceived by others.

Personally, I do all I can to avoid any appearance of impropriety with my students. I never initiate any physical contact in any way. The most physical contact I have with students is when I am high-fiving them or patting them on the shoulder for doing a good job. Also, I do all I can to make sure I am not alone with a student for an extended period of time. If a student approaches me after school asking for help, I will sometimes ask the student to come with me to a colleague's room so I can help him or her in the presence of another adult. If that is not an option, I will make sure to help that student by the open classroom door or in the hallway where we are more visible.

Needless to say, I do not share my personal contact information with my students. When I have students try to friend me on Facebook, I have always respectfully denied their requests. Sometimes students may contact me about a school-related matter via their own email. When I respond, I always cc their parents and/

or my principal to make sure that the communication is not private. When students try to talk to me about very personal information, I usually try to change the subject. If it is more serious personal information, I always tell them to speak with the school counselor or ask the counselor to speak with them.

You may see my behavior as being hypervigilant. You are probably right. I have a need to take these measures in the same way I have a need to make my children put on their seatbelts before we drive. Sure, nothing will probably go wrong if I don't take the extra precautionary step. However, if something does go wrong, the outcome could be tragic.

We have done a good job of addressing what we *should not do* when developing relationships with our students. We now owe it to ourselves to discuss what positive things we *can do* to appropriately build stronger relationships with our students.

There are many things we can do to build bonds effectively and appropriately with our students. Instead of taking interest in a student's social life, we can take an interest in the student's interests. For instance, if a student is a big LeBron James fan, talk to him about LeBron's performance in his last game. If a student is a Harry Potter fan, ask her questions about the books.

Showing interest in students' interests allows us to build bonds with our students. When I first started teaching, I had a student named James, who was a real rebel rouser. He was always off task. He was constantly disrespectful and disruptive. I tried everything to help curb James's behavior. I called home. I sat him away from the students who gave him attention. I gave him detention. Nothing worked.

One day I noticed he had a Philadelphia Eagles football sticker on his copy book. I asked him if he was a fan, and he told me he loved the Eagles. The next day I brought to school an old Randall

Cunningham football card I had when I was a kid. At lunch I called him over and gave him the card. We ate lunch together that day. We talked about the Eagles the whole time. We even debated over who was better, Randall Cunningham or Donovan McNabb.

At the end of lunch, I told him that I thought he was really smart, and I thought he could be a leader in the class. I told him that I needed his help making sure everybody was doing what they needed to succeed. After this conversation, James was the best student in my class and a true leader. He went from being my most disruptive student to my hardest-working student.

Another effective practice is to occasionally make a positive phone call. Many parents of students with academic or behavioral issues are used to receiving emails and phone calls from teachers with bad news. If we take a minute to send the parent good news about their child's behavior or academic performance, it can work wonders.

I had a student named Betsy who was constantly off task and never received anything above a C on any test or quiz. I remember starting a geometry unit with the class. For some reason, she really understood what was going on. She not only knew how to solve the problems, but she also did a great job explaining how to solve the problems to her struggling partner.

After school let out, I took the time to call Betsy's mom to tell her how proud I was of her and how much potential I thought Betsy had. Betsy's mom was both relieved and excited to hear good news come from a teacher. The next day, Betsy came to class with a big smile on her face. She worked hard and acted like a true leader in the class. Clearly, the phone call I made helped motivate Betsy to do better in my class. It also gave Betsy a newfound respect for me. She was motivated to do well in my class because she knew I thought she was smart, and she didn't want to disappoint me.

There are other little things we can do to help build better bonds with students.

They include:

Being approachable
Saying hi to the students as they pass by
Going to students' games and dances
Letting the students know a little bit about your family, where you come from, and what interests you
Showing disappointment instead of anger when a student does the wrong thing
Just being a nice person

Teaching is a wonderful profession. We have the opportunity to build bonds and make an impact on hundreds of children's lives. As professionals, we have to be careful with how we build these bonds with our students. We need to make sure that the relationships are healthy and appropriate.

EAT Notes

E: Have empathy for parents who need and expect teachers to be good mentors their children can look up to.

A: Avoid the uncomfortable conversation with your principal (and maybe even the police) when you explain to them why you shared your personal contact information with a student.

T: Think two steps ahead. If I am acting in such a way that makes it appear that I am more a friend with the students (or a student) than a mentor, what kind of conclusions will people in the school and community draw?

Keep an Eye Out

The job we have as teachers goes far beyond delivering the content of our subject matter. We are also counselors, motivators, disciplinarians, and mentors. Among these duties is the duty we have to protect our students.

The children we teach are more than just pupils. They are all inexperienced and vulnerable young people. This inexperience and vulnerability makes them more susceptible to being mistreated by others. This is why it is our duty to do everything we can to make sure our students are not being bullied or abused.

The next two chapters address the role we take as teachers in ensuring our students' safety inside and outside the classroom.

Chapter 18

Child Abuse and Neglect

Scenario

Mrs. Connie Cerned is a middle school math teacher. She has a student named Brian who she allows to come to her class for tutoring before the school day begins. When he shows up in the morning, Brian always asks Mrs. Cerned if she could give him a snack to eat. He has asked so much that Mrs. Cerned has made it a point to bring in a breakfast bar every morning to give to him.

Brian also tends to miss a good amount of school. Recently, after missing a week of school, Brian came back with a black eye and bruises up and down his arms. When Mrs. Cerned asked him how it happened, Brian said he got the bruises and black eye from wrestling with his little brother.

Case

In *Campbell v. Burton*, an eighth grade student was settling a dispute with another student through her school's peer mediation program.[1] During the mediation, she mentioned to a staff member that she had a family friend who made advances toward her and touched her in an inappropriate manner. The school staff member told the student to stay away from this family friend and advised her to tell her mother about the incident.

The staff member made no attempt to tell school administration or the authorities about the incident. The staff member claimed she did not tell anybody about this because she thought the student was making up stories to get attention. When the abuse suffered by the student came to the surface, her family sued the school district for failing to report it.

Discussion

It goes without saying that a large part of our job is to protect the students we teach. If we suspect that one of our students is being neglected or abused, it is our obligation to report these suspicions. Many schools have a protocol to follow if one does suspect a child is being abused or neglected at home. We should be aware of these protocols if they do exist in our district or at our school.

Look at it from this perspective: no other adult, outside a child's guardians, spends more time with a child than we do. Because of this, we may be the only ones in a position to notice any signs of abuse or neglect. For this reason, we need to keep our eyes open to any signs of abuse. Unlike the person in the case, we need to report what we see and hear to the proper authorities.

As we saw in the scenario, we may find ourselves in a situation where we notice one of our students exhibiting signs of neglect and/or abuse. It is our duty to keep our eyes and ears open to any signs of abuse, and to follow the reporting protocol that exists in our school.

Some signs of abuse include:

Unexplained bruises, bites, burns, and broken bones
Shrinking at the approach of adults
Being frightened by parents
Protesting or crying when it is time to go home

Some signs of neglect include:

Frequent absences
Begging for or stealing food and money
Lacking appropriate medical care
Lacking appropriate clothing
Being consistently dirty or having consistent body odor

I obtained this information from www.childwelfare.gov. It is a great source for information on detecting child abuse and neglect.

EAT Notes

E: Have empathy for a child who is being abused or neglected. Do your part to put an end to their mistreatment.

A: Avoid the uncomfortable conversation with your principal (or the police) when he or she asks you why you didn't report suspected abuse despite the signs.

T: Think two steps ahead. If I say nothing, I may be enabling parents who are abusing their child. This puts me partially at fault for that child's suffering.

CHAPTER 19

Bullying

Scenario

Mr. McFly is a middle school math teacher. He has a student named Brianne in his eighth grade class. He knows her well because she was in his math class when she was in the sixth grade. Mr. McFly remembers Brianne being a very energetic young lady who got very good grades, always helped her peers, and would often volunteer to help Mr. McFly organize his classroom during lunch. She helped him clean his classroom so often, they would joke about how Mr. McFly's classroom would be a mess if it wasn't for Brianne organizing it for him.

In the eighth grade, it was quite a different picture. Brianne wasn't so bubbly. As a matter of fact, she rarely said a word to anybody. Brianne no longer got good grades, and she always seemed unhappy. She wasn't even receptive when Mr. McFly would jokingly bring up how if it wasn't for her, his sixth grade classroom would have been a total mess. Mr. McFly thought little of it. He figured her behavior was just a byproduct of her getting older and becoming a teenager.

Case

To this point, I have given summaries of the facts from the cases we have discussed. However, the case that I am using to address the issue of bullying is different. I feel that for you to completely understand the severity of what occurred in this case, I have to quote the whole factual background from the legal opinion. It reads as follows:[1]

> L.K. was diagnosed with autism spectrum disorder. In 2007–2008, when L.K. was in third grade, she needed substantial adult support to stay on task in class. Her IEP required a 1:1 special education itinerant teacher (SEIT), and speech, physical, and occupational therapy. The record describes several specific incidents and repeated bullying by L.K.'s classmates and limited action by school officials. For example, "J" physically bullied L.K. in May and November 2007 by pinching her hard enough to cause a bruise and "stomp[ing]" on her toes. L.K.'s parents immediately informed school officials of both events, yet the parents were never notified of any action taken, if any, nor did school officials seek information from L.K. or her parents. In another incident, several classmates refused to touch a pencil that L.K. had used. The teacher put a label on the pencil to reflect it was L.K.'s — which ensured the classmates could avoid it. L.K.'s three SEITs testified that classmates constantly teased L.K., including pushing, tripping, or laughing at her, or refusing to have contact with her. One SEIT who began working with L.K. in November 2007 described the classroom at that time as a "hostile environment" for L.K., as L.K. 's classmates ostracized and teased her. Two SEITs stated that L.K.'s classroom teacher ignored their concerns about students' continuous bullying of L.K. In April 2008, a student drew a demeaning picture of L.K. that, among other things, labeled her fat and ugly. The teacher's assistant spoke "brief[ly]" to the student who made the drawing and put the picture in the trash. The SEIT retrieved the picture from the garbage and gave it to L.K.'s parents, which is how they learned

of this incident. L.K. told a SEIT that she was bullied, including being called "fat," "ugly," and "stupid." In May 2008, a neurodevelopmental pediatrician observed that other students constantly ignored L.K. and found that L.K. had "minimal interactions with her classmates, [and t]hese were mostly negative."

As the school year progressed, L.K. became more unhappy, withdrawn, and, as L.K.'s father described, "emotionally unavailable to learn" due to classmates' bullying. L.K. came home crying and complained to her parents on an almost daily basis about being bullied by other students. L.K. was tardy 16 times during the spring semester, twice as many as the fall, due to fear of being ostracized by others. She was absent 15 days in the spring, twice as many days as the fall. In the spring, L.K. brought dolls to school for support on a more frequent basis due to the bullying and ostracism by others. One SEIT explained that the bullying adversely affected L.K.'s "academics, her social, and emotional well-being." Another SEIT reported that L.K. internalizes negative comments by peers, which she has experienced in school this year. Over the course of this academic year, [L.K.] has continuously expressed her sadness, frustration, anxiety, and discomfort with her being bullied. This bullying has negatively affected [L.K.'s] ability to initiate, concentrate, attend and stay on task with her homework assignments and activities after school, which has affected her academic performance [and] negatively affected her confidence and self-image. (The SEIT and L.K. would count the days to the end of the school year).

A doctor familiar with L.K. stated that her behavior had worsened from the prior year. She "seemed anxious, sad, and frustrated [h]er head was often down. She was not volunteering, as she had done last year," and she needed more prompting from an aide. Moreover, the expert observed that the teachers neither intervened nor "deliver[ed] consequences to students." In November 2007, a private physician who knew L.K. for several years assessed her and recommended a different, more supportive educational environment than her current classroom.

Discussion

Bullying is a major issue that plagues our schools. At one time, bullying was considered harmless behavior that was just part of growing up. Now we know otherwise. It is not harmless at all. It is quite dangerous and can cause a great amount of emotional damage to the victim. Because of this, it is our duty to make sure that the children in our care do not become victims of bullying.

Much like the scenario, I found myself in the same position as Mr. McFly. I had a sixth grade student who had all the traits of the "perfect" student. She stayed on top of her studies. She was always completely engaged in my lessons. I would always put her next to a struggling student because I knew she would help them. She would even volunteer to stay at lunch or after school to put papers in student mailboxes or straighten up my shelves.

The following year, I had her in my class again. From the first day, she was a completely different girl. She seemed to no longer care about her studies. She would keep her head down and isolate herself from her peers, and she no longer asked to stay to help me organize my room.

I just figured she was going through one of the many phases that all middle school girls go through. I chalked it up to teenage angst and didn't think much more of it. About three months into the school year, she stopped coming to school. I came to find out that she told her mother that she had suicidal thoughts, so her mom put her in a program where she received the help she needed. Not long afterward, I also came to find that a large amount of her depression came from the fact that she was being bullied by certain students in our school. One of those students sat right next to her in my class.

I felt absolutely terrible. I still do whenever I think about it. I knew something was wrong. It was right in front of me. Instead of calling her parents or talking to one of our counselors at school, I just ignored it and took the easy route. I am still bothered by the fact that her situation may not have gotten to the point it did if I just made one call or sent one email earlier in the school year.

I learned from that experience. I am now much more cognizant of how my students behave, and I tend to assume the worst when a student seems depressed or is not acting like himself. On several occasions when I have noticed a student acting differently, I have told our counselor who talked with the student. I do this because I don't want to make the same mistake again.

It is shocking to see how the teacher reacted to the incidents of bullying that were discussed in the case. I do not want to sound like I am defending the teacher in the case, but she may have gotten caught up in the everyday responsibilities of being an elementary school teacher. Taking time to make sure the students were not bullying each other probably came second to her need to teach her subject matter and manage her class. As we saw with my own situation, it is easy to ignore these issues. Our main responsibilities can take up so much of our time and effort that we have trouble focusing on our other responsibilities.

Much like with the chapter on reporting abuse, we have to remember that we are in a unique position. As teachers, we are probably among only a few adults who see our students for an extended period of time every day. We may be in the best position to take notice if a child is being bullied. This is why we need to be vigilant. We need to keep our eyes open and do what we can to stop bullying when we notice it.

Some signs of bullying include unexplainable injuries, lost or destroyed books or clothing, increased absences, declining grades, and loss of friends. Take a look at www.stopbullying.gov. It is a great site to help you learn how to identify, prevent, and respond to bullying.

EAT Notes

E: Have empathy for the child being bullied. Put yourself in the shoes of a child who is afraid to come to school every day.

A: Avoid the uncomfortable conversation with the principal or parent where you try to explain why you allowed a child to be bullied in your classroom.

T: Think two steps ahead. If you suspect it now and don't do anything, the child's suffering will continue.

Taking Shortcuts

Shortcuts are a part of life. At one time or another, all of us have found and taken an easier route when completing a difficult task.

My brother lives in a fast growing suburb of Philadelphia. It seems that whenever I go to his house, I always get stuck in construction traffic. I remember one day I was traveling to his house for dinner. On this particular day, the traffic was horrible. Because of construction, a two-lane road on the way to my brother's house was reduced to one lane. It caused a major backup. While I was slowly moving in this log jam of cars, I came to an entrance of a new housing development. It was so new that many of the roads in this development weren't completely paved. I knew that if I turned into the development and came out the other side, I could get to my brother's house without having to sit in the traffic.

Needless to say, I decided to do it. I turned into the development and drove through. I had to drive through some very bumpy and muddy dirt roads because only a few of the roads in the development were paved. When I got to my brother's house, my car was a little dirty from the muddy roads, but that was a small sacrifice considering the alternative. The night ended, and I made my way out to my car to go home. As I was approaching, I noticed the car had not one but two flat tires. Apparently, the road I was driving on in the new development was riddled with construction nails. Two of those nails found their way into my tires. It became a huge headache. I had to get the car towed, and I needed to call out of work the next day because I had no way of getting there.

Teaching can be a very time-consuming job. There is nothing wrong with taking the occasional shortcut to make things easier. However, we need to be aware that certain shortcuts aren't worth taking. We don't want to end up like I did that night at my brother's house, when I realized the burden that went along with taking the shortcut far outweighed any benefit it would bring to me.

In the next three chapters, we will explore scenarios where teachers took shortcuts they regretted taking.

CHAPTER 20

Following Student Accommodations

Scenario

Mr. Pederson is a new teacher at Malone Elementary. He feels pretty overwhelmed because he was just hired last week and has a thousand things to do to get ready for the first day of school. At a faculty meeting on the last day before the students are to start school, the principal hands out the BIPs (Behavior Intervention Plans), IEPs (Individual Education Plans), and 504 plans to each teacher for their students. Mr. Pederson has a good amount of students with accommodation plans. The documents stack up to about an inch high. Before dismissing the teachers to go work on their rooms, the principal mentions to the staff that they should make sure to review all the accommodations in the documents.

Mr. Pederson now feels even more overwhelmed. He mentions to the teacher sitting next to him, Mrs. Hakunamatata that he does not know how he will find the time to review all these papers and get done what he needs to finish for the next day. Mrs. Hakunamatata tells him not to worry about it. She has been teaching for years and never reads them. She just files the accommodation plans at the beginning of the year and forgets about them.

It is a few months later, and once again, Mr. Pederson finds himself in a pickle. He has taken a personal day for a doctor's appointment. It is the first personal day he has taken this year. Taking Mrs. Hanunamatata's advice, Mr. Pederson leaves a lesson plan for the substitute and a class list so the substitute can take role. He is hoping he isn't missing anything that the substitute may need.

Case

In *Stewart v. Waco* Independent School District, a high school student had an IEP that addressed multiple impairments.[1] A portion of the IEP provided that she be kept away from male students. It also said that the teachers were to make sure that she was always under close supervision. On several occasions, she was allowed to go to the bathroom alone. During these times, she had sexual encounters with male students. The family was successful in their suit against the school where they claimed the school did not reasonably accommodate their child's needs.

In *Motta v. Board of Education of Law Cruces Public Schools*, the plaintiff was a third grade girl with a medical condition called osteogenesis imperfecta.[2] People who suffer from this condition have extremely brittle bones that are susceptible to breaking. The condition warranted a 504 plan where the child was to be escorted by either her mother or a teacher before and after school. At the end of the day, she was to stay in her classroom and wait for her mother, who was to take her home. On this particular day, the girl left the classroom and did not stay to wait for her mother. While she was walking in the hallway, she slipped and fractured her femur.

The mother of the child sued the school, claiming the teacher was negligent when she let the girl leave the classroom. The court stated, "A reasonable fact finder could find that M.M.'s regular teacher, Mrs. Nelson, was negligent in allowing M.M., a child known to have fragile bones and whose accommodation plan required her to be escorted by an adult when moving about the school, to leave the classroom unescorted by her mother or another adult."

In another case, the plaintiff was a student who was assaulted by a classmate when they were lining up to go to their next class.[3]

The girl who attacked the plaintiff had a history of violent behavior toward teachers and students. The incident occurred in a classroom that was being supervised by a substitute teacher. The substitute teacher was not told about the aggressive girl's behavior. When ruling in favor of the plaintiff, the court noted that the school had a duty to inform the substitute of the girl's violent propensities. If the substitute teacher knew of these behaviors, she could have taken steps to prevent the incident from occurring.

Discussion

Clearly, we should always read and try to understand all BIPs, IEPs, or 504 plans any of our students may have. These documents can be lengthy, but the part that is most important for a teacher to know and understand is where it notes the accommodations that must be given by the teacher to the child. In most cases, the accommodations listed in the plan are short, direct, and easy to understand.

In a regular education class, where the teacher may have a few students with BIPs, IEPs, or 504 plans, the accommodations listed are usually easy to follow. It could be as simple as making sure a child sits in the front of the class or has extra time on quizzes and tests. If you do not read and follow the accommodations, you may find yourself being called into question by a parent or your principal.

I have seen firsthand in parent-teacher conferences where parents ask teachers about specific accommodations that needed to be provided, and the teacher had no idea of what the parent was talking about. When this happens, it makes us look unprepared and unprofessional.

We should take the time to familiarize ourselves with any plans our students may have. It will help us better serve our students and may prevent problems from surfacing in the future.

Personally, I make a short list of the accommodations for my students. I have the names of the students in one column and their accommodations in another column next to their names. It is usually only a two-page document. Whenever I make a call to or have a conference with one of the parents of these students, I will always have the list close by so I can quickly reference the accommodations just in case it comes up in the conversation.

With regard to the situation involving the substitute teacher, we should always relay all relevant information to our substitute regarding any accommodations students may have. Even if the student does not have an individual plan, we should also be sure to notify the substitute teacher of any issue with a student that the substitute will need to know to help maintain a safe classroom environment.

It is always a good idea to relay this information to the substitute teacher in the most efficient manner possible. Many teachers will often leave a copy of all the BIPs, IEPs, and 504 plans with their lessons. We should remember that in many schools, a substitute teacher usually comes into the classroom a few minutes before the bell rings and has little time to prepare for the class with the items we leave them.

It may be a good idea to leave a short list of students with their relevant accommodations. When I say relevant accommodations, I mean the accommodations that the substitute needs to know. For instance, if a student needs extra time on a test, I will not put that on the short list because the substitute will not be giving a test or a quiz. Also, I do not leave information regarding students' seating accommodations because I leave a copy of my class seating chart with instructions to have the students sit in their assigned seats.

I leave notes for the substitute in situations where a child will need to leave the class to go to the school nurse to receive medicine or to use the bathroom. I will also leave notes in situations where certain students should be given verbal instructions or special attention when doing classwork. Furthermore, it is a good idea to include specific strategies for dealing with a child who has behavioral problems.

It is important that we always follow any accommodations listed on any BIP, IEP or 504 plan. Also, if we are not there, we are obligated to make sure that our substitute teacher is prepared to address any specific needs our students may have.

EAT Notes

E: Have empathy for struggling students who need some extra attention to succeed. Do not ignore them or put them to the side.

A: Avoid the uncomfortable conversation with your principal or a parent when you try to explain why you have not been adhering to the requirements of an IEP.

T: Think two steps ahead and understand that if you don't accommodate the needs of that particular student, you may not be helping her to succeed in your class.

CHAPTER 21

Showing a Video to the Class

Scenario

Mrs. Sia Video is a high school history teacher. It is Thursday afternoon. Her last class has just ended, and she plans to take Friday off. Mrs. Video and her husband plan to go on a romantic getaway to a bed-and-breakfast in Vermont. She wants to leave for the trip right after school because she and her husband live a good five hours away from the destination. She is preparing the next day's lesson plans and figures it would be easiest for the substitute to just show a movie to the class. Mrs. Video is presently teaching a unit on the French Revolution. She purchased a short film on the Revolution at a professional development conference she recently attended. It would be much easier for her to leave the movie for the substitute instead of writing out specific plans for each class. Nonetheless, she feels strange letting the kids see the movie because she did not have a chance to preview it.

Case

In *Fowler v. Board of Education of Lincoln County,* the plaintiff wanted to show a movie to her high school class on the last day of school.[1] The movie happened to be *Pink Floyd: The Wall.* Mrs. Fowler never previewed the movie. She did ask a student in the class who saw the movie if there were any parts that should not be shown. He said there was one bad part that students shouldn't see. She did show the movie and the student covered the screen during that scene. The movie did have a good amount of nudity, sex, and violence in it.

When the school board found out that she had shown the movie, she was fired for conduct unbecoming of a teacher. Mrs. Fowler sued the school, claiming that her First Amendment freedom of expression rights were violated. The appellate court disagreed with her. It reasoned that Mrs. Fowler did have the "academic freedom to exercise professional judgment in selecting topics and materials for use" in her class.[2] However, she also has the responsibility of instilling the "fundamental values necessary to the maintenance of a democratic political system."[2] Showing movies that can be offensive to people infringes upon this responsibility.

Discussion

As we have seen in the scenario and the case, it is not uncommon for teachers to show a video or movie to their students at the end of the year or before a long holiday. I believe using videos is a great tool to help the students stay engaged. If another person can deliver a lesson better than I can, why shouldn't I show the video of that person giving that lesson? Also, if a person or a cable channel put together an awesome presentation on what I want to teach, it would be foolish of me not to show that presentation, especially if that presentation is much more engaging than anything I could do.

Many of us will often include a video as part of a lesson that we leave for a substitute. In these situations, it is often very easy for a teacher to have the students watch some video to keep their attention and prevent disruptive behavior. I have a couple of videos in my own small video library that I or my substitute can show the students on any particular day.

That said, we need to take caution with regard to what we decide to show the students. If there is a school or district policy that addresses the showing of movies to students, we should know and follow the policy. Prior to showing a video, inquire with your principal and be sure to check your teacher handbook or district policy. In addition to any specific requirements that may already be established by the school or district, it may be wise to take the following steps.

We should always preview the video. Do not trust what another person might say about the movie. As we have seen in *Fowler,* it is a bad idea to ask a student about the content of a movie and rely on their answer without checking it out ourselves. I knew a teacher who was given a movie by his district office to show his students in his history class. He showed the movie to his class without previewing it because he presumed somebody in the district office must have watched the movie before approving it for use. He was wrong. There was a good amount of nudity and foul language in the movie. At certain points, he actually had to jump in front of the screen as the movie was playing so the students would not see what was happening. Luckily, he did not get any complaints. It is a good idea to make sure we always preview a movie or video before we show it to our students.

After previewing the movie, we may want to make our principal aware of our intentions to show the movie, especially if it contains offensive or controversial subject matter. If we feel strongly about showing a movie that may offend some people, we may also want to send a letter home to parents that describes the movie and asks for permission to have their children see it.

I have another friend who is a language arts teacher. She teaches a unit on the book *Lord of the Flies*. She shows clips from the movie as part of one of the lessons in the unit. Because some may hesitate to have their 12-year-old child see the movie, she sends a letter home to parents that describes the scenes being shown and asks permission to show the specific scenes to the child. She also recommends that the parents watch the movie if they have not already seen it.

Also, some people may take offense to material that others may consider harmless. One year on Halloween, I remember my school had an assembly at the end of the school day. During that hour, they showed some funny Halloween-themed cartoons. The next day, an upset parent showed up at the principal's office, complaining about the movie. Apparently, his family was very religious, and his church did not believe in celebrating Halloween in any way. By showing the cartoon, he believed that we were forcing his child to celebrate the holiday. A letter home to this parent prior to showing the movie would have prevented this from happening.

For many teachers, showing a video is an easy way to captivate the class. Oftentimes it works as a great classroom manager if it is late in the year or if a substitute is in the room. However, we should always take the proper precautions before showing a video.

EAT Notes

E: Have empathy for the parents who do not want their child to see material that they consider offensive.

A: Avoid the uncomfortable conversation with the principal or a parent where you are trying to explain why you didn't preview a movie that had inappropriate content.

T: Think two steps ahead. If I show this movie without previewing it and it contains an offensive scene, I may be held to blame by parents and administrators.

CHAPTER 22

Peer Grading

Scenario

Ms. Dela Gate is a new fifth grade teacher at the local public elementary school. As with many new teachers, she finds herself overwhelmed with little to no time to take care of her responsibilities. She spends several hours a night planning for the next day's classes. Ms. Gate spends so much time lesson planning, she does not have much time to do the other things that teachers need to do, like contacting parents, grading class work, and organizing her classroom. It is not uncommon for her to be up until 1:00 a.m. grading tests that were given a week before. In addition to this, on her first day of work the principal pulled her into the office and told her that she was in charge of the yearbook. Ms. Gate is completely overwhelmed, the school year is not even halfway complete, and she is already feeling burned out.

In the teacher's lounge, Ms. Gate is venting about her situation to another fifth grade teacher in the school, Mr. Connie Fidential. Mr. Fidential is one of those happy-go-lucky guys who has been teaching for 15 years and never seems to be stressed by anything. He told her that he has a personal policy never to do schoolwork at home. He makes sure he has time to go to the gym every other day and coach his son's basketball team at night.

Naturally, she asks him how he can do that considering she barely has time to eat dinner. Mr. Fidential gives her some really good tricks of the trade to help her be more efficient with her time. He also tells her that he barely has to do any grading. When his class completes a test or quiz, he just has the students switch papers with the person next to them. He then reads out the answers, and the students mark the tests for him. They even put the grade at the top of the paper for him. All he has to do is look at the grades and log them into his gradebook. Ms. Gate loves this idea. It would save her hours of work if she did this. Yet, she feels like this may not be a proper way of going about doing things because the students would be seeing each other's grades.

Case

In *Owasso Independent School District No. 1011 v. Falvo*, the court had to decide whether a graded test or quiz could be considered an "education record" for purposes of FERPA (Family Educational Rights and Privacy Act).[1] FERPA is a privacy law that forbids schools from sharing certain parts of students' educational records. The facts of the case mirror the facts in the scenario. A parent asked her child's school to ban the practice of peer grading because it was embarrassing to her child. When the school declined her request, she sued, claiming the practice of peer grading violated FERPA.

The case went all the way to the United States Supreme Court. The mother argued that the tests and quizzes that were being graded by the other students were part of her daughter's "educational record." Therefore, it was information that could not be shared with others by the school without her permission. In its ruling, the court disagreed. It concluded that the score did not become an "educational record" until it was put into the grade book by the teacher.

Discussion

Even though the court did rule that peer grading did not violate FERPA, I believe we should avoid this practice in our classroom.

The benefit of the saved time may not outweigh the burden of having to deal with the issues that may arise when we use peer grading.

First, there are many students who, for whatever reason, do not like others to know their grades. These are the kids who you see grab their test and immediately put it in their folder when you hand it back to them. When a sensitive student gets a bad grade, there is no reason to make the disappointment of receiving the bad grade even worse by having his classmate grade the paper and see the grade. By doing this, we also may be inadvertently contributing to a bullying situation. Imagine if you have a bully or a friend of the bully grade the test of a sensitive student who fails the test. Common sense dictates that the bully's knowledge of the other student's poor grades can only make things worse for that student.

Also, peer grading may help a teacher save time, but I can safely say that the likelihood of making a grading mistake will increase exponentially if the students are doing the grading as opposed to the teacher. Imagine yourself in the principal's office with an upset parent. It seems that the grade you gave her daughter was lower than it should have been because the student grading her test was not paying attention and marked several correct answers wrong. It will not look good if you try to explain to the parent and the principal that it was not you who made the mistake, but it was the mistake of the classmate who sat next to the student.

Better yet, imagine yourself in the same situation, but the parent is upset because the student who grades her daughter's paper is making fun of her because all of her answers on the last quiz were wrong. The mother will surely ask you and your principal why you allow students to grade each other's tests. I can promise you that if we tell her that we do this to help save time, it will not fly with either party. We will end up looking a little lazy and very inconsiderate.

Again, I strongly recommend that we do not use peer grading when it comes to quizzes and tests. Nonetheless, in certain situations, there is justification to having students share their work. In my opinion, it is good practice to have students share and discuss their work with items that we use as part of a lesson. A teacher is justified in doing this because the items are not being graded and there is a pedagogical purpose to it.

There are many things we can do to help save time. We just have to make sure that the shortcuts we take do not compromise the quality of our work.

EAT Notes

E: Empathize with the student who is sensitive to having his grades seen by other students.

A: Avoid the uncomfortable conversation with a parent who is upset because your practice of peer grading has contributed to a bullying situation.

Conclusion

I felt the need to write this book because there is really nothing much out there to help direct teachers when they encounter those moments where their small decisions could have huge consequences. Of course, the situations we have discussed do not completely cover every situation you will encounter or have encountered in your career. If I wanted to, I could have added many more cases where teachers made decisions they shouldn't have made. For your sake and mine, I limited it to the 22 scenarios that I felt to be the most important.

If we look at these chapters as one cohesive piece of work, we can see certain patterns in teacher behavior. In every case, the teachers displayed a lack of empathy, they didn't think two steps ahead, and they didn't think how their choices would force them to defend an indefensible decision. This is why I believe if we keep these three things in mind (having empathy, avoiding the awkward moment, and thinking two steps ahead), we will be better equipped to make good decisions in our careers as educators.

But it really is much simpler than this. All we have to do is use a little common sense. Common sense is not like money, where some people have it and others don't. We all have it. It is more a matter of when we decide to use it. People who tend to make good decisions are just more in tune with their common sense. It is my hope that the discussions in this book will help us better recognize those moments in our professional lives when we just need to use a little common sense.

Endnotes

Introduction

1- Philip Wesley Jackson, *Life in Classrooms*. (New York: Teachers College Press, 1990), 149.

Supervision

Chapter 1: Supervising the Classroom

1- *Flanagan v. Canton Central School District*, 871 N.Y.S.2d 775, 58 A.D. 3d 1047 (App. Div. 2009).

2- *Cirillo v. City of Milwaukee*, 34 Wis. 2d 705, 150 N.W.2d 460 (Wis.1967).

Chapter 2: Line Them Up and Watch the Halls

1- *Purzycki v. Fairfield*, 244 Conn. 101, 708 A. 2d 937 (Conn. 1998).

2- *Bonamico v. Middletown*, 47 Conn. App. 758, 706 A.2d 1386 (Conn. App. Ct. 1998).

Chapter 3: Field Trip Supervision

1- *Glankler v. Rapides Parish Sch. Bd*, 610 So.2d 1020 (La. Ct. App. 1992)

2- *The Estate of Anthony v. USC Shen Win Chinese Inst.*, Cal., Los Angeles County Super. Ct., No. KC 038 483 (2003).

3- *Bell v. Board of Education*, 665 N.Y.S.2d 42, **687 N.E.2d 1325** (App. Div. 1997).

Chapter 4: The School Bus

1- *Doe v. DeSoto Parish School Board,* 907 So. 2d 275 (La. Ct. App. 2005).

After School

Chapter 5: Leaving Students Alone After School

1- *Broward County School Dist. V. Ruiz* 493 So. 2d 474 (Fla. Dist. Ct. App. 1996)

Chapter 6: Passing a Child to the Right Person

1- *Baker v. Clay*, 871 F. Supp. 930 (E.D. Ky. 1994)

Chapter 7: Keeping a Student after School

1- Philip Wesley Jackson, *Life in Classrooms.* (New York: Teachers College Press, 1990), 149.

Student Expression

Chapter 8: The Pledge of Allegiance

1- *West Virginia Board of Education v. Barnette* 319 U.S. 624 (1943).

2- Id at 642

Chapter 9: Student Expression in Class Papers

1- *Lacks v. Ferguson Reorganized School District R-2*, 147 F.3d 718 (8th Cir. 1998).

2- *Bethel School District v. Fraser*, 478 U.S. 675 (1986) at 681.

Chapter 10: Cyber-Bullying of Teachers

1- *Killion v. Franklin Regional School District*, 136 F. Supp. 2d 446 (W.D. Pa. 2001).

2- *J.S. v. Bethlehem Area School District*, 757 A.2d 412 (Pa. Commw. Ct. 2002).

Know the Policy

Chapter 11: Following the Dress Code

1- *Guiles v. Marineau*, 461 F.3d 320 (2d Cir. 2006) at p. 322.

Chapter 12: Giving Homework

1- *Gilliland v. Board of Education*, 67 Ill. 2d 143, 365 N.E. 2d 322 (1977).

2- Mike Horsley and Richard Walker. Reforming Homework: Practices, Learning and Policy (South Yarra, Palgrave Macmillan, 2012).

Chapter 13: Grading Policy

1- *Keen v. Penson*, 970 F.2d 252 (7th Cir. 1992).

Be Aware

1- Philip Wesley Jackson, *Life in Classrooms*. (New York: Teachers College Press, 1990), 149.

Chapter 14: Student Bathroom Use

1- *Boyett v. Tomberlin* 678 So. 2d 124 (Ala. Civ. App. 1995).

2- Id. at 125.

3- Id at 127.

Chapter 15: Use of Social Media

1- *In the Matter of Tenure of Hearing of O'Brien,* No. A-2452-11T4, 2013 WL 1321508 (N.J. Sup. App. Div. 2013)

2- Id

3- Id

Chapter 16: Giving Food to Students

1- *Soter v. Cowles Publishing Company,* 174 P.3d 60 (Wash. 2007).

2- *Pace v. State,* 425 Md. 145, 38 A.3d 418 (Md. 2012)

Chapter 17: Student-Teacher Relationship

1- *Doe v. Tippecanoe School Corporation et al,* No. 4:15-CV-56-RL-PRC, Document 57 (N.D. Ind. 2017).

Keep an Eye Out

Chapter 18: Child Abuse and Neglect

1- *Campbell v. Burton,* 92 Ohio St.3d 336, 750 N.E.2d 539 (Ohio 2001).

Chapter 19: Bullying

1- *T.K. v. N.Y.C. Dept. of Educ.,* No. 14-3078 (2d Cir. 2016).

Taking Shortcuts

Chapter 20: Following Student Accommodations

1- *Stewart v. Waco Indep. Sch. Dist.*, 711 F.3d 513 (5th Cir. Tex. 2013).

2- *Mata v. Bd. of Educ. of Las Cruces Pub. Sch.*, No. 12-CV-00136 MCA/SMV (D.N.M. May. 21, 2013).

3- Id. at 4

4- *Ferraro v. Board of Education*, NYC, 32 Misc. 2d 563 (NY Sup. Ct. 1961).

Chapter 21: Showing a Video to the Class

1- *Fowler v. Board of Education of Lincoln County*, 819 F.2d 657 (6th Cir. 1987).

2- Id. at 661.

Chapter 22: Peer Grading

1- *Owasso Independent School District No. 1011 v. Falvo*, 534 U.S. 426 (2002) *citing* The Family Educaitonal Rights and Privacy Act, 20 U.S.C. § 1232g; 34 CFR Part 99 (1974).

About the Author

Mike Burger is a math teacher in Southern Delaware. Mike grew up in Philadelphia where he learned to become an avid Philadelphia sports fan. He graduated from Temple University in 1994 with a degree in political science. He went on to law school with the intent of becoming a trial lawyer. In 1998, Mike graduated law school and began his legal career. Mike married his beautiful wife, Jill, in 2002. When his first son was born in 2004, Mike decided to give up his law career to become a teacher. Mike will tell you it was the best career move he ever made.

Mike has taught at the elementary and middle-school level. He is presently teaching 5th grade math. Mike has also worked as an adjunct professor at Wilmington University and has given numerous seminars on avoiding the pitfalls of the teaching profession. In his spare time Mike enjoys hanging out with his family at the beach and being a dad to his two teenage sons, Tyler and Zachary.